Frank George Carpenter

Carpenter's Geographical Reader

South America

Frank George Carpenter

Carpenter's Geographical Reader
South America

ISBN/EAN: 9783337370053

Printed in Europe, USA, Canada, Australia, Japan

Cover: Foto ©Andreas Hilbeck / pixelio.de

More available books at **www.hansebooks.com**

CARPENTER'S GEOGRAPHICAL READER

SOUTH AMERICA

BY

FRANK G. CARPENTER

NEW YORK .:. CINCINNATI .:. CHICAGO
AMERICAN BOOK COMPANY

PREFACE.

IN this book the children are taken by the author upon a personally conducted tour through the most characteristic parts of the South American continent. Leaving New York, they sail through the Atlantic Ocean and Caribbean Sea to the Isthmus of Panama. Here they cross over to the Pacific, and travel along the west coast, visiting all the different countries and learning about their civilization and industries.

They climb the Andes; they explore the highlands of Ecuador, Peru, and Bolivia, and steam over Lake Titicaca. They travel extensively upon the great coast desert, visit the wheat and fruit lands of Chile, and then make their way about through the Strait of Magellan into the Atlantic.

They go along the Atlantic coast, through Patagonia, into the pastures and pampas of Argentina, and sail on the Parana and Paraguay rivers for thousands of miles into the heart of the continent.

Returning through the Rio de la Plata, they make their way along the coast of Brazil to the mouth of the Amazon. They explore the wilds of the great Amazon valley, and then go on into Venezuela to the Orinoco river, down which they sail into the Atlantic, and close their tour with travels in Dutch, French, and English Guiana.

Among the striking features of the book are the pictures of life and work among the people of the various countries. The children take journeys through the cities; they see life in the villages, and spend days upon the farms, in the factories, and in the mines, seeing all phases of life among the rich and the poor, the savage and the civilized.

The great industries of South America have received especial attention. In the Andes the young readers go down into the mines and see how gold, silver, and tin are extracted from the earth. They explore the nitrate fields on the coast, see the great borax lakes of Bolivia, examine the guano islands, and are carried out under the ocean into the subterranean coal mines of southern Chile.

They learn about sheep raising during their travels in Tierra del Fuego and Patagonia, and upon the pampas of Argentina they visit the greatest stock ranches of the world. They travel through the coffee plantations of Brazil, and spend some time in the rubber camps of the Amazon and in the cacao orchards of Venezuela and Ecuador.

They learn much of the curious animals of the different zones, and see the wonders of nature in the flowers and trees of the tropics.

The travels are in the shape of an imaginary tour made by the children themselves, with the author as a guide. The book will, it is believed, aid in putting flesh and blood on the bones of the geographies, and will give a living interest to geographical study.

The book has the merit of being written from original sources of information. It comprises the observations of the author gathered in a trip of more than twenty-five thousand miles along the routes herein described. Most of the descriptions were written on the ground, and a very large number of the photographs were made by the author especially for this book.

CONTENTS.

		PAGE
I.	From New York to Panama	9
II.	The Isthmus of Panama	16
III.	Across Panama to the Pacific	24
IV.	The Republic of Colombia	29
V.	The Land of the Equator	38
VI.	The Great South American Desert	50
VII.	In Lima, the Capital of Peru	58
VIII.	Up the Andes	67
IX.	On the Roof of South America	72
X.	Steamboating above the Clouds	81
XI.	Travels in Bolivia	87
XII.	The Mineral Wealth of the Andes	95
XIII.	On the Nitrate Desert and the Guano Islands	100
XIV.	Along the Coast to Valparaiso	108
XV.	Across South America by Rail	115
XVI.	Santiago, the Capital of Chile	123
XVII.	A Visit to a Chilean Farm	130
XVIII.	Southern Chile and the Araucanians	137
XIX.	In the Coal Mines of Chile	144
XX.	In and about the Strait of Magellan	151
XXI.	At the End of the Continent	159
XXII.	In Argentina—Patagonia	167
XXIII.	In Argentina—Life on the Pampas	174
XXIV.	In the Great Fruit and Bread Lands of South America	182

CONTENTS.

		PAGE
XXV.	In Buenos Aires	192
XXVI.	Uruguay—In Montevideo, the Paris of South America	201
XXVII.	Up the Rio de la Plata System	208
XXVIII.	In Paraguay	218
XXIX.	Paraguay—A Trip into the Interior	226
XXX.	Paraguay—A Curious Tea—The Chaco and its Indians	233
XXXI.	In Brazil—The Wilds of Matto Grosso	243
XXXII.	Southern Brazil	249
XXXIII.	In the Land of Coffee	257
XXXIV.	Rio de Janeiro	267
XXXV.	More about Rio	274
XXXVI.	Bahia and the Diamond Mines	283
XXXVII.	Along the Coast of Brazil	291
XXXVIII.	The Valley of the Amazon	299
XXXIX.	Para, the Metropolis of the Amazon	305
XL.	In the Land of Rubber	312
XLI.	A Trip on the Amazon	320
XLII.	On the Orinoco and the Llanos	327
XLIII.	Venezuela and its Capital	334
XLIV.	In the Guianas	342
	Index	351

LIST OF MAPS.

South America	*Frontispiece*
Isthmus of Panama	18
Colombia	30
Peru and Bolivia	73
Tierra del Fuego	158
Argentina and Chile	202
Brazil	242
Venezuela and Guiana	343

TRAVELS THROUGH
SOUTH AMERICA.

I. FROM NEW YORK TO PANAMA.

IT is a great undertaking to explore a whole continent, but that is what I shall ask the boys and girls to do with me in this book. We shall travel together over all South America, to learn what kind of a country it is and what it has in it, and to see for ourselves just what is going on in every part of it.

We shall first sail from New York to the Isthmus of Panama, and crossing that narrow neck of land, go through the Pacific Ocean along the west coast to the Strait of Magellan, stopping here and there, and making many trips far into the interior. We shall go through the strait about the southern end of Patagonia, and then travel along the east coast of the continent through the Atlantic to the mouth of the Amazon, journeying thousands of miles inward at different points, and exploring all the great rivers. From far up the Amazon we shall go north through the wilds into the lands along the Caribbean Sea, and thence take ship for New York.

This will be a very long journey. South America is so large that we must travel much farther than the distance around the world if we would visit only its principal parts. It is a difficult trip. Much of it will be in the Andes Mountains, which are among the highest on earth, and in Argentina we shall travel over plains and pastures where for thousands of miles we shall not see a hill.

We shall find all kinds of animals and, I might almost say, all kinds of men. There are curious Indians here and there over South America; there are mixed races in most of the states; and there are numerous negroes, as well as several varieties of the Caucasian race. Many of the people have odd customs, and we shall find everything strange.

But our steamer, the *Alliança*, for the Isthmus of Panama, is lying at its wharf in New York, ready to start. I

"Our steamer is ready to start."

wonder if we are well prepared for the journey. Let us look carefully over our baggage and see. It will be hard to buy things in some of the countries, for we must remember that but few South American cities have so good stores as we have.

It is now winter. It is so cold in New York that we dare not go out on the street without heavy clothing. We shall be in the land of perpetual summer when we step from the steamer upon the Isthmus of Panama, and our overcoats and flannels will seem very hot on the equator. And still we cannot throw them away, for we shall need them in cold Patagonia and while we are climbing the snowy peaks of the Andes. No; our first business is to lay in a good stock of all kinds of clothing.

Another thing which each of us needs is a good saddle and bridle. Many of the journeys will be on donkeys and mules, and the saddles sold in South America are very uncomfortable. I think the boys should take guns, for we may have shots at alligators and jaguars, at tapirs, and perhaps at peccaries or wild hogs.

We also need cameras and photographic supplies to bring back records of the things we see, in order to prove that the stories we tell are founded on truth.

But stop a moment. I wonder if we all have our passports. There are often revolutions in South America, and during such it is not the easiest thing in the world to keep one's head on one's shoulders or to keep out of prison. We must be able to prove that we are Americans, so that we can claim the protection and rights that our citizens have all over the world.

Passports are furnished for this purpose by the Secretary of State at Washington. Each passport is a piece of white paper about as large as a sheet of foolscap, certifying

A Passport.

that its owner is an American citizen. It has the coat of arms of the United States at the top, and at the bottom the big red seal of the State Department at Washington. Between the two there is a description of the person to whom the passport is given. It tells just how tall he is, the color of his eyes, hair, and face, whether his nose, chin, and mouth are big or little, and just how old he was when the passport was issued. It also bears his signature. The paper is signed by the Secretary of State, and it requests all people to permit the bearer, who is a citizen of the United States, safely and freely to pass, and in case of need to give him all lawful aid and protection.

We find our passports all right, and are counting over our baggage when we are warned that it is time to be off. The ship has already finished loading its cargo, and we make our way in and out among the men who are wheeling on board the bags containing the South American mails.

A moment later the bell rings to notify all who are not going with us to leave. There are farewell kisses and hurried good-bys. The engines begin to throb, and as we wave our handkerchiefs to our friends on the wharf our boat moves slowly out into the East river and down by Staten Island through the harbor of New York.

Within a short time the city has passed out of view, and as evening falls we stand at the stern of the steamer and watch the lights of Sandy Hook fade away into the darkness, realizing that we shall not see our native land for many months to come.

It is about two thousand miles from New York to Colon', on the Isthmus of Panama; but our ship does not go so fast as the big steamers of the Atlantic, and it takes a full week for our voyage.

The first day out is cold and bracing, and we spend the time in learning our steamer. It is a ship of three thousand tons, about fifty feet wide and three hundred feet long. It flies the American flag. The sailors are from different parts of New England, and our captain is a Yankee from Maine. At high noon every day he makes an observation, telling by the sun just where we are, and a little later on we all rush to the cabin to learn how many miles we have gone in the twenty-four hours.

"At high noon he makes an observation."

At the close of the second day the air becomes warm. We are crossing the Gulf Stream, that mighty river of the Atlantic which is three thousand times as great as the Mississippi in volume. The water is now warmer than that of the ocean through which it is flowing. It warms the air like a furnace, and we can feel the difference as we pass out of it and travel along its eastern edge toward the Caribbean Sea.

But why do we not keep in the stream and be warm all the way?

You will easily see when you remember how hard it is to pull a boat against a strong current. The Gulf Stream flows northward at the rate of three miles an hour, and we are going as fast as we can to the south. If we should keep in the stream we should have to steam against a three-mile current, and we should lose at least three miles an hour.

We find the weather much colder outside the stream. It is not long before it grows warmer, however, for we are sailing southward and shall soon be in the Caribbean Sea. It is already so pleasant that we can leave off our overcoats, and we walk the deck, scanning the wide expanse of blue water on all sides.

But what is that away off to our right? It is little more than a blue speck in the distance.

That is one of the most famous islands in the world. It is San Salvador, upon which Columbus landed when he first discovered America. The sight that greets our eyes is the same that greeted his more than four hundred years ago. When he first stood upon San Salvador he thought it an island off the coast of Asia, and did not realize that he had discovered a new world. San Salvador is one of the most fertile of the Bahamas. It produces fruits, grain, and roots in great abundance, and it is as rich to-day as it was when Columbus landed upon it.

A little farther south we see a white lighthouse standing among a grove of palm trees, and the captain tells us we are looking at Bird Rock Island, another of the Bahamas; and still farther south the bleak and rocky coasts of eastern Cuba come into view, with the purple mountains of Haiti in plain sight on the opposite side of the ship. We sail between these two islands for hours, and then go out over the blue waters of the Caribbean.

The sea is now like glass. The sun is quite hot at noon, but during the rest of the day the air is soft, warm, and pleasant. It is like a June day in Ohio. We put on our thin linen clothes and enjoy our voyage over the tropical seas.

We sail for two days with no land in sight. There are few ships, and the only moving things upon the waters are the gulls which hover about us and the schools of flying fish which dart from wave to wave, one now and then jumping too high and lighting on our deck in its flight.

But listen. The captain calls out that we are approaching the Isthmus of Panama. We are coming near to that wonderful strip of earth and rock which ties North and South America together.

We rush to the prow of the ship and look toward the west. At last a thin, hazy line of blue floats up out of the waters at the horizon. Now the blue deepens. It rises up in the form of low mountains, while little green islands bob out of the sea in front of our ship.

Now we are still closer. See, there is a low city along the shore. It is surrounded by green trees and plants, and rising out of it and over it are tall palm trees with fanlike leaves moving to and fro in the breeze. That town is Colon, the city at the eastern end of the Panama Railroad, where we are to land, and those trees are real cocoanut palms, which seem to be waving to us a welcome to the Isthmus of Panama.

II. THE ISTHMUS OF PANAMA.

WE shall cross the Isthmus of Panama on a railroad in a very few hours. The first white man who went over took twenty-nine days, and his journey made him famous for all time as one of the world's great discoverers.

It was only a few years after Columbus discovered America. Then no one knew that this land was an isthmus. Most people supposed it to be a part of Asia. Expeditions were being made to learn just what the land contained, and among the explorers was a young Spaniard named Vasco Nuñez de Balboa, who came with a party to the Gulf of Darien, not far south of Colon. Here he founded a settlement and went out among the Indians trading for gold.

One day when he was weighing some gold which he was about to buy, a young Indian chief struck the scales with his fist, scattering the precious metal upon the ground, and said:

"If this is what you prize so much that you are ready to leave home and risk your lives for it, I can tell you of a land where gold is as cheap as iron—where it is so common that the people eat and drink out of vessels made of it."

What the Indian said was true. He spoke of Peru, a country which was then rich in gold, and in which we shall travel by and by.

His saying excited Balboa, and he questioned the chief, who told him that the land of gold lay to the westward over the mountains, where there was a sea so great that no one had ever come to its end.

Balboa then decided to find out if this story were true, and on September 1, 1513, he started. It took him eleven days to cut his way through the thick forest to the top of the mountains, and then on the 25th of September, 1513, he saw a great sea to the south, which he called the South Sea, but which we call the Pacific Ocean. Four days later he climbed down the west slope, and with sword in hand rushed into the waters up to his waist, and claimed the great sea and all it contained for the King of Spain.

The Isthmus of Panama is not large. The neck of an hourglass is not so narrow in comparison with the globes which it joins as this little neck of land with the continents of North and South America above and below it.

At its narrowest part, if it were level, we could walk across it in a day, while to cross North America from New York to San Francisco requires six days and nights on a fast railroad train, and in South America to make our way from the Atlantic up the Amazon as far as we could go, and thence to the Pacific by land, would take more than two months.

Yes, the isthmus is very narrow, but it forms a great wall against the commerce of the world. See those boxes and bales of goods which are being taken out of the hold of our steamer. They are putting them on the cars which will carry them across to the city of Panama, on the Pacific. There they will again be loaded upon ships going north to San Francisco or south to Ecuador, Peru, and Chile. Those men who are working must be paid, and the railroad charges high prices for freight. Indeed, the transfer of goods across the isthmus costs so much that it is often cheaper to send them from New York to San Francisco on ships clear around South America, although the distance is eight thousand miles greater.

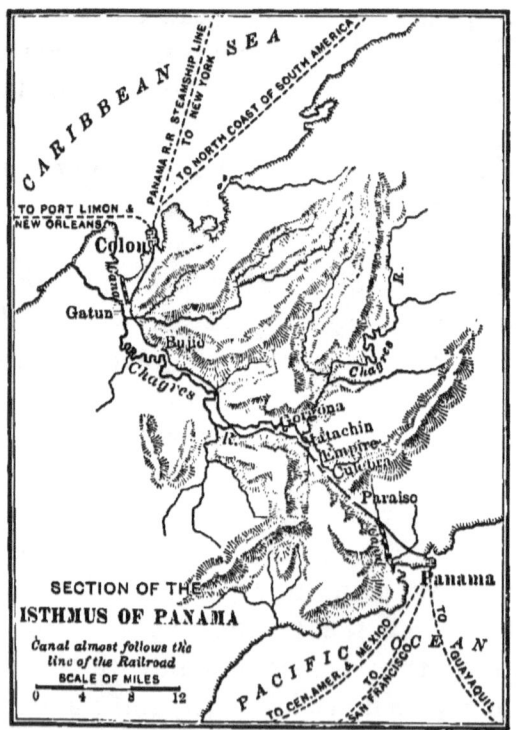

What a fine thing it would be if we had a canal cut across the isthmus wide enough for the biggest ships to sail through! Then our Pacific coast, Hawaii, and the Philippines would be thousands of miles nearer by ship to our Atlantic coast; and Europe and Asia, so far as commerce is concerned, would be much closer together.

Such canals have been planned ever since Balboa showed that the two great oceans at this place are so close to each other. There are now two great undertakings to cut through the land from one ocean to the other. One is the Nicaragua Canal across Central America by way of the large Lake of Nicaragua and the river San Juan, and the other is the canal which is being dug by the French from Colon, where we now are, to the Bay of Panama, on the Pacific.

We shall see much of the Panama Canal as we cross on the railroad. Vast sums have been spent upon it, but it is still far from completion. We shall see what a great job it is to cut through the land, although at this point the isthmus is so narrow that one of our fastest trains might cross from ocean to ocean in an hour.

The chief obstacle is the series of great mountain chains which runs north and south along the west side of our hemisphere from Alaska to the Strait of Magellan. We knew of it in the Rockies and the Andes. It exists also at the Isthmus of Panama, although it sinks so low at this place that the greatest peaks are not half a mile high. Indeed, the pass through which the canal is to go is only two and one half times as high as the Washington Monument. Still, the mountains are masses of rock, and it takes a long time, by blasting and drilling and dredging, to cut them down so as to make a ditch wide enough and deep enough for ships to pass through.

Another difficulty in making the canal is in the great rains. The isthmus is one of the rainiest parts of the world, and during some of the year the streams and rivers flowing down the mountains become raging torrents. The Cha'gres river, which crosses the line of the canal, sometimes rises in one rainy night as high as a four-story house, so that it will take a great dam to hold back its waters. Indeed, it will cost so much to make the canal that many people wonder if it will be completed.

But we have some time yet before the train starts, and we can take a run through Colon. We cross the track of the Panama Railroad, which runs through the town, and visit the entrance to the canal, where we see great dredges and numerous small boats. The dredges are idle and covered with rust. There is a vast amount of machinery

"The dredges are idle."

going to ruin, for the work in this part of the canal has been given up for the time.

We learn that Colon was largely made by the canal people, and that the most of the men we see on the streets came here to work upon it. Among them are negroes from Jamaica who address us in English, and brown-faced Colombians who speak nothing but Spanish. The Colombians are the descendants of the Spaniards who came here centuries ago. Some of them are pure whites, and others are of the mixed race of Spaniards and Indians.

Colon has also a sprinkling of French, Americans, and English. It has many Chinese, the first of whom were brought here by the thousands years ago to work on the

Front Street, Colon.

railroad. They did not get along well, and so many of them died that one of the stations on the railroad is called Matachin', which, freely translated, means "dead Chinamen."

What a queer town Colon is! We say this again and

again as we walk through its streets. Many of the houses are empty, and nearly all are going to ruin. When the canal was started, thousands of people were employed upon it, and it was thought that Colon would be a great city. The finest part of it was made for the officers of the canal, and was called, after Columbus, the town of Christophe Colomb.

We take carriages and drive through this section. Its wide streets are lined with cocoa palm trees, each of which has a bushel or so of green cocoanuts hanging close

"We take carriages and drive through this section."

to its trunk where the leaves jut out. The cocoanuts are as big as the heads of the half-naked negro babies who are playing under the trees, and we think that a commotion would arise if one should drop down among them.

We see more cocoanut trees as we drive through other parts of Colon. They are found almost everywhere on the isthmus. The most of them are wild, but there are also cocoanut plantations where we can learn just how the trees grow. They are so easy to raise that we almost wish we could stop and start a grove of our own.

The cocoanut trees are first sprouted by placing a lot of the nuts on top of the ground, a few inches apart. After a while each nut sends out a sprout from one of the little eyes at its end. The sprout grows up into the air, and at the same time a root shoots out of its base down into the ground.

Within a few months the sprout has grown as high as a table. The sprout and nut are now broken off from the root and set out where the tree is to stand. The nut is buried about six inches deep in the ground, the rest of the sprout remaining above. The earth is pressed tightly down about the sprout, and the planting is done.

Cocoanut trees are set out at about the same distance apart as the trees of our peach orchards. They grow rapidly, and at seven years begin to bear nuts. The fruit ripens all the year round, and we see blossoms and nuts on the same tree.

The nuts are not picked from the trees, but they drop when they are ripe. The men go daily from tree to tree to gather the nuts. Each nut has a thick green husk upon it. This is torn off, and the nuts then look as we see them in our stores, and are ready for shipment.

They are loading cocoanuts on the steamer when we get back to the wharves. The captain will take a shipload to New York, and tells us that they will be sold there by the thousand for two or three cents apiece.

III. ACROSS PANAMA TO THE PACIFIC.

OUR train for Panama is ready to start. We buy our tickets of an American station agent, and later on we notice that the conductors and other railroad officials are Americans. The Panama Railroad was built by Americans shortly after gold was discovered in California. It has been very profitable, although it has cost a great deal of money and thousands of lives. Indeed, so many men died of fever while working upon it that it is said there was more than one death for every tie in the track.

The cars are much like our cars at home. Each seat has its window, and we have a good view of the country as the train whirls us along through tropical wonders.

Now we go by a banana plantation. See how the wide

Banana Peddlers.

green leaves of the plants extend up from the ground higher than the head of a man. They are nearly as high as the top of the cars, and great bunches of green bananas bend down among them, almost touching the ground.

Now we pass orange trees loaded with fruit, and there is a tree filled with green and ripe lemons. There are many forest trees, the names of which we do not know. Some of the trees are covered with orchids, and some are masses of other beautiful flowers. Among them are fern trees, and also bamboos of many varieties, which wave their tall, green, feathery branches in the breeze made by the train as we pass.

There are twenty different varieties of palms on the isthmus, some of which are of wonderful value. That small, fat, bunchy tree, with the leaves sticking out on all sides, is the ivory palm. See those prickly green balls, as big as your head, which grow close to its trunk at the top. In those balls are the nuts which form the vegetable ivory of commerce. Each nut is somewhat like a chestnut, but about five times as big. That train which is passing us now is probably carrying thousands of ivory nuts to Colon, whence they will be shipped to New York, and there made into buttons, combs, and other such things.

Sago Palm.

But see, there is another strange palm. I mean that one at your left, with the green shoots at the top. That is the cabbage palm. Its head looks like a cabbage, and if you should cook it you would find that it tastes much the same. On the hill farther back there are palms which furnish the sago we cook in puddings and soups, and now and then we pass what the natives call the wine palm, because from its sap they can make a sweet drink which will intoxicate like wine.

But we are coming into the mountains. We are slowly climbing the hills. There are woods all about us. The forests in the distance look more like the woodlands of our country than those of the tropics. The trees are closer together, and they are so bound about with vines that we could not make our way through them without chopping it out with an ax.

We see but few birds, as they are frightened off by the noise of the train; but a short distance back from the railroad there are bright-colored parrots and great scarlet-breasted toucans with bills four inches long. There are yellow birds about as big as a robin, which whistle like mocking birds, and orioles whose beautifully woven nests hang down like bags from the trees.

Cocoa Palms and Cocoanut.

There are also many wild animals. See that monkey which is grinning at us out of the branches of that tree as we pass. There are monkeys of all sizes on the isthmus, as well as ant-eaters, jaguars, and wild hogs.

There are snakes, large and small, from the poisonous

viper to the great boa constrictor. There are plenty of insects. We must be careful where we walk, lest we step on a tarantula, a scorpion, or a centiped.

Notice the telegraph poles. They are made of iron. This is because of the ants, some of which eat wood. These ants sometimes travel in armies, and they will consume a pine telegraph pole in a night.

The mosquitoes are worse than ours of New Jersey, and I warn you to beware of a little insect called the chigoe, or jigger, which attacks the bare toes just under the nail. When it bites you it will not hurt more than the prick of a needle, and the bite will make only a little red spot on your toe. As it bites, however, it lays its eggs in the little hole it makes in the flesh. The eggs are so small that you can hardly see them, but if you do not soon dig them out with a needle they will hatch into worms, which will cause you great pain and probably the loss of your toe.

The isthmus has many varieties of lizards. We see them crawling out from under the

Iguana Lizard.

ties on the railroad, and we may have a chance to eat them when asked out to dine. The flesh of one variety of lizard is as tender as a spring chicken. It is sold in the Panama markets. This is the iguana lizard. It is from three to six feet in length, and its eggs are of the size of a marble. The eggs are yellow and shriveled, but are by no means unpalatable.

But here we are on the other side of the mountains. We go quickly down to the lowlands, and end our journey in Panama, with the Pacific Ocean before us.

Panama has about twenty-five thousand people. It is one of the most picturesque cities of the hemisphere. Its houses are built like those of old Spain, with galleries

Wharves, Panama.

hanging out, so that we are shaded from the sun as we walk through the streets. The streets go up hill and down. They wind in and out around a great bay which is guarded from the sea by green islands.

There are many good stores, and several hotels. We visit the wharves and see the great business that is done in transferring goods from one ocean to the other. We spend some time on the bay looking at the ships which have

Cathedral, Panama.

come from different parts of the world. They are anchored far out from the shore, at the edge of the islands, on account of the tides, which are here very strong. We learn that one is just about to sail southward along the coast of Colombia, and upon it we take passage.

IV. THE REPUBLIC OF COLOMBIA.

WE are sailing southward this morning upon the mighty Pacific. Were it not for the slight breeze of the northeast trade winds it would be stifling, and as it is the sea seems to steam.

Come with me to the side of the ship and look out to the west. Notice how the blue waves stretch on and on until they lose themselves in the sky. We are on the greatest of the oceans. That water extends westward for ten thousand miles until it wraps itself around the Philippine Islands and washes the east coast of Asia.

Colombia.

How bright the sun is, and how dazzling! It darts its rays down, and millions of diamonds are dancing upon the waves under our eyes. We wink and blink as we look. The reflected rays of the sun are here as bright as its direct rays in July at our homes.

Come now to the other side of the vessel and look at the shadows. The water below us is of an indigo blue, which seems to grow lighter as our eyes travel over it to the green hills of the shore.

What is that cackling and crowing and quacking we hear? Can that be the baa of a lamb? Was not that the moo of a cow? We rub our eyes to see if we are not dreaming. This voyage of ours must be a mistake, and we are surely back near one of the farmyards in the country at home.

No, it is not a mistake. The noise of the fowls comes from those two-storied coops on the deck. You can see the chickens and geese poking their heads through the slats. The bleating and mooing is from sheep and cattle which are kept in stalls two floors below. They are carried to furnish the meat for our tables. It is so warm here on the southern Pacific that fresh meat will soon spoil.

What a noise the creatures make! We are awakened by them every morning, and hardly know where we are until the cabin boy brings in our breakfast. It consists of a small cup of coffee and one or two slices of bread, and protest as we may, we cannot have more until eleven o'clock. This is the custom throughout South America. Between eleven and one they have a second breakfast, which is much like our dinner, and their dinner is at about six in the evening. We grumble at first, but soon find it is as pleasant as our way of eating at home.

But here we are sailing into one of the ports of Colombia. There are palm trees and bamboos on the coast, and the dense vegetation is much like that of the isthmus. There is a town a little back from the water. It is composed of thatched huts and of one-story white buildings covered with plaster and roofed with red tiles. There are some little sailing vessels at anchor, and many small boats in which dark-skinned men are rowing out to the steamer. We are now in the Bay of Buenaventura (boo-a-nä-ventoo'rä), and from here we shall make a long tour through Colombia.

The country is so vast that we cannot expect to visit it all. Colombia is ten times as large as the state of New York. It is as long from north to south as the distance from St. Paul to New Orleans, and its coast line on the Caribbean Sea is longer than the distance from New York to Chicago.

It is a land of mountains and plains. The Andes run through it in three high ranges, and between them are some of the most fertile river valleys of all South America. The mountains contain many rich mines of silver and gold. There are men from all parts of the world digging the precious stuff out of the hills, and there are some places in which diamonds are found mixed with the gold. Colombia has produced more than six hundred million dollars' worth of gold.

We make our way over the coast range of the Andes from Buenaventura, traveling for the first twenty-five miles upon a little narrow gauge railroad, and then taking mules.

The animals carry us on their backs up one steep trail after another, and bring us at last into a region said to be one of the most healthful and beautiful on earth. This is the valley of the Cauca river. It is covered with plantations of sugar cane, coffee, and cacao. There are great fields of bananas and large orange orchards. There are many lemons, and we make lemonade of the fruit which we ourselves pull from the trees.

Cacao

We stay for a day with a farmer to see his cacao plantation. The cacao tree bears the fruit from the seeds of which our chocolate is made. The planter has thousands of trees, and upon our mules we ride with him through one cacao orchard after another. How beautiful everything is! The trees look like lilac bushes, except that they are from fifteen to thirty feet high. They are ragged and gnarly. Their leaves are of a bright green, and the fruit is so large that if it lay on the ground you might think it a little squash or a very big ripe cucumber. It is of a bright lemon color, streaked with red. It grows close to the bark of the trunk and branches, and not on the ends of twigs like apples or pears.

At our request the planter gives us a specimen. We chop it in two with a knife. It has a thick skin, and inside this a white pulp in which are imbedded about thirty dark-brown seeds much like large lima beans. From these seeds are made the chocolate and cocoa of commerce.

The fruit is gathered when ripe, and the seeds are washed out of the pulp. They are dried in the sun and shipped to factories in different parts of the world. In the factories they are ground, and from their meal, after several processes which take out some of the oil, the pure chocolate is made. From the seed hulls, in much the same way, cocoa is made.

In another part of the plantation we learn how the trees

Village in Colombia.

are grown. The seeds are first planted in hills about fifteen feet apart, three seeds being put in each hill. They soon sprout up, and at first look not unlike small orange trees. They are cultivated, and the weeds are kept down. At three or four years they begin to produce fruit, and continue to yield for thirty years and more.

We see many cacao orchards in other parts of Colombia, and we learn that raising this product forms one of the great South American industries. We shall find other orchards in Ecuador and in the lands farther east. Indeed, a great deal of the chocolate which is drunk in the United States and Europe comes from this part of the world.

We are delighted with the people of the Cauca valley. They are noted for their hospitality, and are so kind that

Capitol, Bogota.

their country has been called "The Land of the Gentle Yes," because the people hate to say no to any request. They are largely composed of the mixed race of Spaniards and Indians. They are very simple in their tastes, their chief business being farming and fruit raising.

We take boats and sail for days down the Cauca river, coming at last into the Magdalena river, where we find steamers bound for Honda, the port from which Bogotá, the capital, is reached.

Honda is as far from the mouth of the Magdalena as Pittsburg is from New York, but the river extends southward many miles farther. It is a vast stream more than a thousand miles long, forming the great internal highway of Colombia. We sail through the lowlands, winding this way and that across the stream, avoiding the sand bars. We pass

Cargo Boat.

many river steamers loaded with freight, and cargo boats with negroes and Indians, who stand upon them and push them onward with poles which they thrust down into the bed of the river.

Farther north the scenery grows grander. We are now near high mountains, and at Honda, a small river town, where we land, we take mules and climb for two days up the steep roads which lead to the great plain upon which Bogota is situated.

Bogota is one of the high cities of the world. It is

almost nine thousand feet above the sea, or much higher than Denver or Mexico city. As we rise we find the air cooler. On the Magdalena the heat was intense, the very water was warm, and at Honda the stones were almost too hot to touch. At Bogota we are in a temperate climate, fresh and cool in the daytime, but so chilly at night that when we go outside the hotel we wear overcoats.

We spend some time in Bogota, studying the city and people. It has about one hundred thousand inhabitants, the most of whom are of the mixed Spanish and Indian race.

Bogota is a Spanish-built town. Nearly all the houses are of one story, close to the street, with iron bars over their windows. They are painted in the brightest of colors, and nearly all have roofs of red tiles.

The best part of the city is about the Plaza Bolivar (bō-lē'var), a beautiful park with gardens of flowers and tropical trees. On one side of the plaza is the capitol, or government building; and on another, with arcades before them, are stores containing goods from all parts of the world. We see many people out shopping. The ladies are dressed in black, with black shawls over their heads, but the men of the better classes are dressed like our men at home.

We are surprised to find that Bogota has street cars, public libraries, and schools. It has telephones and electric lights, and it has daily newspapers printed in Spanish. In it are the houses of Congress and the homes and offices of the president and other officials who govern the Republic of Colombia. There are many soldiers, and we are awakened each morning by the trumpeters who are calling the troops out to drill.

The strangest things to us, however, are the Indians and

the donkeys. The Indians dress in cotton. The men have on white shirts and trousers, and sometimes also a poncho, or blanket, which they wear over their shoulders,

Indian Women.

sticking their heads through a hole in the center. The women wear dark clothes, and nearly all have on straw hats like those our boys wear in the summer.

The donkeys are the beasts of burden of the city. They take the place of carts and wagons. Bread, vegetables, and fruit are carried about from house to house upon them, and at the market scores of these little animals stand and wait while their masters sell the produce they have brought in from the country.

We see more donkeys and Indians as we go back to the

seacoast over the mountains. Our journey is made upon mules, and it takes a long time for us to climb the two ranges of the Andes between Bogota and the Pacific.

Mat Makers.

At last, however, we reach Buenaventura, and are glad to be again in our cabins, hearing the throb, throb, throb of the huge engine as it forces the vessel through the ocean. We pass the southern boundary of Colombia, and then coast for a time along northern Ecuador. As we cross the equator the sun grows hotter and hotter, and we feel almost roasting as we enter the great Gulf of Guayaquil (gwi-ä kĕl′) and sail up the Guayas river to Guayaquil, the chief seaport of Ecuador.

V. THE LAND OF THE EQUATOR.

ECUADOR means equator, and we are now in one of the lands of the equator. Ecuador lies on both sides of that central line of the earth. It is of the shape of a fan, whose handle extends almost to Brazil, and whose scalloped rim is fringed with the ocean spray.

The exact size of Ecuador is unsettled. According to the boundaries which the natives claim, it is larger than Texas; but if Peru and Colombia are allowed what they assert belongs to them it will be but little larger than Colorado.

It is a curious country, made up of lowlands and highlands. The parts of it along the coast and near the east boundary are low and tropical, and the remainder is a land of the clouds. It comprises some of the highest of the Andes, with mighty plateaus where the climate is cool and temperate, and where in some parts it is perpetual spring.

We are now in the most tropical part of the country. Guayaquil never needs a furnace, and heating stoves are unknown. Look at the city as it lies there on the banks of the river. There is not a chimney rising above any of the houses. There is not a stovepipe in the city, and the weather is so warm that most of the buildings are made without windows, mere holes in the walls serving for light and air.

The boatmen who have rowed out to the ship to take us on shore are half naked, and as we land at the wharf we see half-naked babies playing about near their mothers, who sit there peddling oranges, pineapples, bananas, and all sorts of tropical fruits.

How the sun beats down upon us as we stand in the street, and what a vile smell comes up from the gutters! Guayaquil is very unhealthful; it often has yellow fever; and we must be careful to keep out of the sun. Let us go farther over into the business part of the city. Now we are walking under arcades by one great store after another. It is like passing through a museum or a bazaar of East India. The stores are all open. The front walls

Street Scene, Guayaquil.

have been folded back or taken away for the day, and the goods are piled upon the counters and stacked upon the floors.

What a queer throng is this that moves along in the shade! There are women dressed in black, with black shawls over their heads. There are Indian girls from the interior, in bright-colored gowns and straw hats, and there are dark-faced Indian peons, or workmen, who trot along with great bags of cacao and other things on their backs.

What a lot of donkeys there are in the street! There is one loaded with lumber. Three long boards have been strapped to each of his sides, and he clears the whole street when his master turns him about. There is another donkey with two large wooden boxes slung over his back. That is the bread wagon of Guayaquil, and that boy who is dragging him onward is probably the son of the baker. There are other donkeys carrying vegetables in panniers, and we see that donkeys and mules here take the places of our huckster carts, carriages, and drays.

"The bread wagon of Guayaquil."

But what is the matter with that donkey's legs? He is actually wearing trousers. There is also a band of cotton cloth on the under part of his body. There are other donkeys dressed the same way. We ask why this is, and are told that the flies and gnats are so bad in Guayaquil that the donkeys have to wear waistbands and trousers.

Let us take a walk through the streets. They are lined with workmen, who are laboring at their trades on the sidewalks, and Indian women, who comb their own and their children's hair as they wait for their customers.

We stop a moment before a house which is just being built. The carpenters are nailing bamboo laths on the framework of the building, and spreading upon them a thin coat of plaster. The part of the house they have finished looks as though it were made of brick or stone covered with stucco, when in fact it is so thin that you could ram a hole through it with a rail. See how the beams and rafters are made in sections and spliced. The houses are so constructed on account of the earthquakes which are felt here every few weeks. Heavy buildings will fall if the earth shakes very much, but these light structures thus put together sway to and fro, but do not come down.

Guayaquil is quite a business center. It is one of the best ports on the west coast of South America. It lies about sixty miles up the Guayas river, where the stream is a mile wide, and so deep that it furnishes a safe harbor for great ocean steamers. The river is filled with shipping, and there are many dugouts and cargo boats which have brought goods — cacao, cane sugar, and ivory nuts — from the interior of Ecuador for shipment abroad.

There are also little steamers which take us up the Guayas river almost to the foot of the Andes. We leave at night, and awake to find ourselves floating in and out among houses built high upon piles surrounded by water. It is the rainy season of Ecuador, and the low coast lands are flooded. The people of this region are now living in the second stories of their houses. We see them going from one hut to another in canoes. There are marketmen paddling about, and there is a group of children in that little boat being paddled to school.

The town at which we now are is Bodegas (bo-dā'gas). It is the head of navigation of the Guayas river. Only a small part of it is on the mainland, and this part is half flooded, so that the street crossings are bridged with logs, and the people have to hug the walls and step upon blocks in getting from one store to another along the side streets.

Many of the houses are far out in the river. The smaller ones have only one room, made of poles covered with palm leaves, and reached by ladders from the water.

"Many of the houses are far out in the river."

Let us take a canoe and visit one of them. The owner makes us welcome, and we squat down on a block on the floor, sitting rather gingerly upon it for fear the floor may break through and drop us down into the water. See, it is made of bamboo canes. There are so many cracks that the women do not need to sweep, for the dirt falls through into the river, or to the ground during the dry season.

Notice that clay pot resting over the little fire in that box over there. That is the cook stove of the family. These people use charcoal for fuel. They live largely upon sweet potatoes or yams, plantains or large bananas, and a potatolike tuber called the yucca. They are fond of rice, and eat a great deal of beef dried in the sun.

Leaving Bodegas, we start out for our trip over the Andes. We ride for miles in canoes through the flooded lands, among the treetops of the tropical forest. Now we pass alligators, which swim lazily off into the bushes. Now monkeys make faces at us out of the branches, and now a bright-colored parrot shrieks out as we go on our way. We take a shot now and then at an alligator, but fail to hit the beast in a vulnerable spot.

We pass many Indians in canoes and flatboats, carrying their wares down to Bodegas. We ride by cacao plantations, and finally shoot out of the woods into the open, with the mighty Andes rising above us.

Now we have left the river and are on our mules, climbing the mountains. The road is so narrow in places that we have to go single file, and so steep now and then that we fear we shall slip off behind. Now we ford a stream, throwing our legs high on the donkey's neck to keep our feet out of the water, and now we go along narrow ledges, shuddering to think how we should be dashed to pieces if the little animals should slip in the mud. The roads grow worse farther up, and we heartily agree with the natives of the country who say that their roads are rather for birds than for men.

As we ride higher still the air becomes fresher and colder. We are now out of the region of coffee and cacao, and in one of less luxurious vegetation. We have left the tropical forests, and at last reach a point so far above the sea that there are no trees at all.

We shiver under the blankets in the rude huts where we stay overnight, and find our accommodations very uncomfortable. Our beds are on wooden platforms. We are tormented with insects, and at one place the chickens, cats, and dogs run in and out of the rooms where we are trying to sleep.

Farther on we come to a plain higher up in the air than Pikes Peak. It is covered with sand, and the cold wind almost blows us from our mules as we attempt to ride over it. This is the Arenal, the pass of the Andes through

Village in the Andes.

which we reach the high central valley which forms the chief part of Ecuador.

Now we have gone through the pass and are on our way up through the valley toward Quito. We are almost two miles above the sea, with some of the highest of the Andes about us. Over there is Chimborazo, its snowy peak kissing the clouds more than four miles above Guayaquil; and on each side of us, extending up and down the valley as far as our eyes can reach, are great mountain peaks, many of which are three or four miles in height.

The great valley of Ecuador extends through the country from north to south, with these mighty mountains on each side of it. Some of the mountains are active volcanoes. We see the vapor rising from them as we ride onward. There are frequent earthquakes in this region, and the houses are built to withstand them.

The high valley of Ecuador is a rich farming region. We ride through fields of potatoes, barley, and wheat, passing orchards and gardens, and green clover fields in which cattle are feeding. We go from one small town to another until we come to the little city of Ambato, where we get the stage for Quito. In this we go on the gallop all day long, changing our mules now and then, until at last we reach the capital of Ecuador.

We are now in the highest capital city of the world. Quito is more than a thousand feet higher than Mount Saint Bernard, the highest point in Europe upon which men can live throughout the whole year, and the place where the famous Saint Bernard dogs are kept to hunt for men lost in the snow.

Climbing the Andes.

On Saint Bernard there is often ice all the year round. We find no ice at Quito. The air is as warm as that of May in our northern States, and the people tell us that their climate is perpetual spring. The great height so tem-

Chimborazo.

pers the heat rays of the sun as to make them just right, although the city is almost on the equator. We enjoy the clear sky and the fresh air from the great mountains about, and learn to prepare for the showers which come regularly during about two hours every afternoon.

Quito is an odd city. It has fifty thousand people. The streets are laid out at right angles. They are so narrow that there is room for little more than foot passengers. Most of the people walk or ride on mules and horses, and almost all carrying of goods through the city is upon donkeys or mules.

The houses of Quito are of one or two stories, made of stone or bricks covered with stucco, and roofed with red tiles. A large part of the town is given up to convents and churches, and we see priests, clad in white and in black gowns, going about everywhere.

There are many women dressed in black, with black shawls on their heads, going to and fro, and crowds of queer Indians who have come in from the country. The Indians have on bright-colored costumes, each tribe having a style of its own.

Ecuador has a great many Indians. More than two thirds of the population, it is said, are of the red race. The majority of the Indians are semicivilized. They have small farms, or work for the whites and mixed race of Spaniards and Indians. These people are the descendants of those ruled by the Incas at the time the Spaniards first came. They had approached nearer to civilization than the Indians of the lowlands, and had covered this valley between the ranges of the Andes with their cities and villages.

One of the largest cities was Quito, a much greater town then than it is now. In it Atahualpa (ä-tä-hwäl'pä), the Inca monarch, had a palace whose roof was covered with gold, and there were many other fine houses.

The Spaniards under Pizarro conquered Atahualpa and made the Indians their slaves. Other Spaniards came afterwards; some of them married with the Indians, and the descendants of the Spaniards and of the Spaniards and Indians form the ruling classes in Ecuador to-day.

The pure Indians are still little more than the slaves of the whites. They till the soil. They carry boxes of goods on their backs up

Uncivilized Indians.

and down the mountains, and do all kinds of hard labor for small pay. They are not thrifty, and do not seem to care that they are in debt to their masters, who can therefore force them to work. They seem to have no ambition whatever. If one of them has a little brick or stone hut, a suit or two of cotton clothes, and a little rice and meat, with enough money to enable him to get drunk now and then, he considers himself very well off.

Not all the Indians in Ecuador are civilized. Some whom we see in Quito have very hard faces. They have come on long journeys from the eastern part of the country, bringing skins and other things from the wilds to the markets for sale. Among them are Indians who have a horrible practice of curing the heads of the enemies they kill. They cut off the head and, having removed the bones, fill the skin with hot pebbles to dry it. As it shrinks they keep pressing it inward on all sides so carefully that it does not lose its shape, but dries up to the size of a man's fist, keeping the same features it had when in life. Such heads are sometimes baked in the sand, and when so treated they will last for years. They are grewsome objects, and when an Indian takes us aside and offers to sell us one, which he pulls from under his blanket, we turn away in disgust.

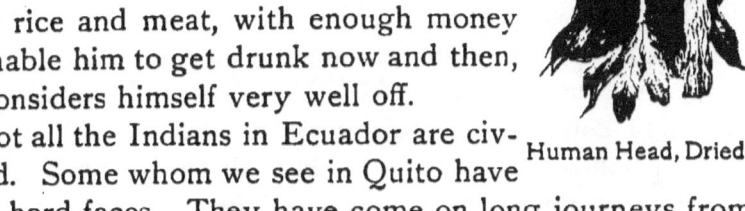

Human Head, Dried.

Water Carrier.

There is a university in Quito, and in our trips through the country we find here and there a public school. We can always tell where they are, for the children study out loud, often making such a din that they can be heard a long distance. We learn, however, that only a small portion of the people can read, and that the majority of the children do not attend school. This condition will probably be bettered, for although Ecuador is one of the most backward of the South American countries, it is slowly improving.

A railroad has been planned from the coast up the Andes to Quito. A part of it is already built, and the day may come when this temperate valley, with its rich farming lands, will be connected with the seaport by rail.

At present the only way to and from Guayaquil is by mule, and we must travel back in the same way we came.

VI. THE GREAT SOUTH AMERICAN DESERT.

WE have left Ecuador and are now in the coast lands of Peru. We are in the midst of the great South American desert, which extends from Ecuador two thousand miles south along the coast of Peru and Chile. As far as we can see to the north and south there is nothing but sand, sand, sand. On the east the thirsty foothills of the Andes rise and lose themselves in gray rocky mountains, which, piled one above another, end at last in perpetual snow. On the west are the sparkling waters of the Pacific, casting their silvery spray upon the beach. The air is cool and dry, but the sand is so dazzling under the rays of the sun that we shield our eyes with smoked spectacles to keep out the glare.

In the coast lands of Ecuador the soil was black and moist, and the tropical vegetation so thick that we had to chop our way a foot at a time to get through it. Here we gallop on our horses for miles without seeing a tree, a flower, or a blade of grass.

Now we pass queerly shaped hills which seem to be in motion, and which really are moving toward the north. These are the traveling sand dunes of Peru. They are of the shape of a half-moon and are of different sizes, some so small that they could be put into a schoolroom, and others so large that they contain many hundreds of tons of this traveling sand.

Traveling Sand Dunes.

But how can a hill travel? Come to one of the sand mounds and see. The coast winds, which here blow almost always toward the north, roll the little grains on the south side of the pile over one another, so that they travel up the outside of the half-moon and roll down on the inside, keeping the hill of the same shape, but slowly moving it onward.

The traveling sands cover up everything they meet. They hide the bridle paths, which are the only roads of the desert, and for this reason we dare not go without a guide, who directs our course by the stars at night and tells us where we are by the winds during the day.

Now we see the skull of a traveler who has been lost and has died here, and now and then a flock of vultures picking at the bones of animals which have perished of thirst in the desert; now a mighty condor, the biggest bird that flies, circles high in the air above us, making a moving shadow on the plain; but for most of the time there is nothing but sand and rock and sea.

Is not this a wonderful region? Yes; but it is easy to see that it cannot be otherwise when we think just where it is. First, let us remember that the atmosphere is the clothing of the earth, and that old Mother Earth works well only when her clothes are periodically wet. We also know that the mountains are the great clothes wringers of nature. They squeeze the water out of the air which comes against them, and by the differences in temperature cause it to fall upon the land.

Now, the chief winds which sweep over the South American continent come from the east. They start from the hot shores of Africa across the warm regions of the South Atlantic. They pump themselves full of water as they cross the ocean, so that when they reach the coast of Brazil they are well loaded. As they go over the land they are somewhat cooled, and drop some of their burden in the form of rain, feeding the great rivers of eastern South America, and covering the land with tropical verdure.

They drop more and more water as they climb up the

eastern slopes of the Andes, so that when they have reached the top almost all has been squeezed out, and what is left falls there in snow. These winds then sweep on along the Pacific. They are cold, but so dry that they have not a drop left for the coast. The result is a desert upon which rain seldom falls.

And are there no oases in this great desert? Yes; here and there, at wide distances apart, we find little rivers made by the melting snows of the Andes. There are in the whole two thousand miles of sand about forty such streams, and along them are the only places where people live. It is in these snow-water valleys that Lima, the capital of Peru, and other quite large cities are located, and here are some of the best farm lands of Peru. The soil of the desert is rich, and if water can be got to it it will produce almost any kind of crops. We ride out of the sands into irrigated fields, and are surprised to see the rich plantations of sugar cane, rice, tobacco, and cotton which grow here, with nothing but sand all about them.

We come upon vineyards, in which delicious grapes hang from the vines, and we slake our thirst with oranges which we pick from the trees. There are no better fruit lands anywhere than the irrigated

Papaw Tree.

valleys of this sandy region. Bananas, oranges, limes, and lemons grow side by side with peaches and pears, and there are delicious cherries, plums, dates, and figs. There are watermelons and muskmelons, guavas and mangoes, and also papaws and alligator pears. The papaw is a fruit as large as a muskmelon and grows on a tree, and the alligator pear, which is not so large as our pears at home, has a flesh that tastes like fresh butter, and is eaten with salt. We find fruit for sale in every town, and for a very few cents we can buy all we can eat.

The farms are divided into small fields, fenced with thick walls of mud as high as your waist, and are covered with a network of ditches to water the crops.

In the north, in the Piura valley, there are rich fields of cotton, much of the cotton wool being red or brown instead of white like ours. Peru raises fine cotton. If the plants are allowed to grow they become trees and produce small crops of cotton for ten years. The cotton plant blooms throughout most of the year, and we see buds, blossoms, and cotton wool on the same tree at the same time. The best of the cotton is grown on plants only one or two years old. It is more like wool than ordinary cotton, and is used by the manufacturers of hats, stockings, and underclothes to mix with wool, as it renders the articles less liable to shrink.

There are many sugar estates in the valleys farther south. Sugar cane is one of the chief crops of Peru. The cane is much like our Indian corn. It is planted in rows, and comes up so luxuriantly that the fields in the distance seem a mass of beautiful green. Some of the plantations are large and well worked. Many of the rich farmers use steam plows and harrows, and the cane is hauled from the fields to the sugar mills upon little railroads.

Most of the farming, however, is done in a small way. The fields are cultivated with oxen yoked to the plows by their horns. They do little more than scratch the ground as they drag the plow over it.

The larger farms are owned by the rich whites or by people of the mixed race of Spaniards and Indians. Those who do the work are the Indians, who, from their lack of ambition, and from the laws which make those in debt work for their creditors, are little more than the slaves of the

Peons in Ponchos and Rebosas.

whites. The peons, as these people are often called, receive very low wages, but seem to be perfectly satisfied with their lot. They are very ignorant, and but few know how to read.

There is a group of them now at work in that field.

They are as brown as our Indians, although they do not look at all savage. Both women and men wear straw hats. The men have on leather sandals, but the women and children are barefooted. They dress in that way all the year round, except when it is cold and on Sundays and feast days. Then the men wear ponchos over their shoulders, and the women have rebosas draped about their shoulders and heads.

We shall see ponchos and rebosas nearly everywhere on the west coast of the continent. The poncho is the overcoat and dress coat of the native man. It is merely a bright-colored blanket as large as a bed blanket, with a hole in the middle. You stick your head through the hole and allow the folds to come down over your shoulders. It looks quite picturesque, and it is both warm and comfortable. The rebosa is a long black shawl large enough to cover the shoulders and at the same time to be wrapped around the head.

But let us enter the hut of one of the peons and learn how they live. The hut is made of cane, and we can see out on all sides through the cracks in the walls. The floor is the ground, and the roof is of reeds, for it is needed only to keep out the sun, there being no danger of rain on the desert. The house has only one room, which is not so large as many a room in our houses at home.

Where is the furniture? It looks as if the people had moved, for there is not much to be seen. There in the corner is a wooden platform as high as your knee. That is the sleeping place for the father and mother. The children sleep on the floor. There are no mattresses, no blankets, and no quilts. Each peon wears at night the same clothing he has on during the day, the little ones huddling together to keep warm when the nights are cold.

Look at the opposite corner. See those two stones placed just wide enough apart to allow that earthen pot to rest on them. That is the cooking stove for the family. In preparing the meals a fire will be placed under it, and thus the stew of goat's meat and rice, the most common food, will be cooked. The house has neither windows nor chimneys, and, with the exception of that rude box over there, no furniture at all. This Indian has a few chickens and goats. You can see them now outside the hut. At night he will bring them indoors, and animals and family will all rest together.

We shall find such Indians over all Peru, although their houses and clothes will be warmer in the cold lands of the mountains. They are of the same race as the Indians we saw in the highlands of Ecuador, and we can hardly realize that they once owned the whole country and that they were more civilized in some ways than their descendants are to-day. We shall see the ruins of their large cities and villages, and discover evidences that they once farmed a vast territory which is now nothing but desert and waste. They knew how to irrigate the soil. They even cultivated the hillsides of the Andes. There are still terraces high up in the mountains which they cut out and built up with earth to raise crops.

These Indians were a very rich people, and their rulers really did eat and drink from dishes of gold and silver, just as the Indian chief told Balboa. Their Spanish conquerors took out of one of their temples, it is said, as much gold as forty-two horses could haul at one time, and about twice as much silver. The silver nails of another temple weighed twenty-two thousand ounces, and there was so much more silver that when the horses of the invaders needed new shoes they were shod with this precious white metal.

The leader of the Spaniards was named Pizarro. He was a cruel man, and acted dishonestly with the Indians and with the Inca king, their ruler. After he had got possession of the king by inviting him to take supper with him in his fortress, he closed the gates and killed the king's attendants. He then fought the Indian army, which was thus without a commander, and conquered it. He kept the king in prison, but told him he would release him if his subjects would fill the room in which he was imprisoned with gold from the floor to a mark on the wall as high up as a man could reach. The king sent this word out over the land by messengers. A vast amount of gold was brought, and then Pizarro, instead of allowing the king to go free, had him condemned to death and cruelly killed.

The Spaniards soon became masters of the whole country. For centuries after this time they treated the Indians with the greatest cruelty. They made slaves of them, forcing them to work in the mines. They used them so badly that many died, so that to-day Peru, with both white people and Indians, has not so many inhabitants as it had when the Spaniards first came.

VII. IN LIMA, THE CAPITAL OF PERU.

LET us climb to the roof of our hotel and take a bird's-eye view of the Peruvian capital before we begin to explore it. We are in a vast field of flat roofs, above which, here and there, rise the massive towers of great churches. At the back are the bleak foothills of the Andes, gray and forbidding. There are white clouds rushing over their sides, and the hills rise one above the other until they lose themselves in the dark, smoky sky. This morning the tops of the Andes are hidden. On

"At the back are the bleak foothills of the Andes."

bright days their snowy summits, glistening in the sunlight, shine like masses of silver high above Lima.

Turn your eyes again to the city. See that rushing stream which flows through it. That is the Rimac (rē'-mac) river, which has come from the tops of the Andes to water this beautiful valley, whose green fields stretch away beyond the houses to the right and left.

It is this river that makes Lima possible. Without it all would be desert. It waters the large plantations of sugar, cotton, and other rich crops which extend from here six miles to the east, where the river flows into the sea.

With a glass we can see the Pacific. That town on the coast is Callao (cäl-lä′ō), the seaport of the capital and the chief port of Peru, and that train which is rushing down through the green fields is carrying passengers and freight from Lima to the steamers.

What queer roofs these are all about us! They are more like little gardens than the coverings of houses. Please step more lightly, and do not stamp your feet as you walk to and fro. The roof is trembling under us, and with a little effort we could push our way through. The roof is made of bamboo poles, with earth spread upon them. Were it not for the plaster, the dust would sift through into the rooms. It is so with the most of the other houses about us, some being covered with canes, upon which matting is spread, and upon that a layer of earth, sand, or ashes.

Is not this a strange way to build houses? You would think all would melt through if it rains. Yes, so it would, but we must not forget where we are. We are in the great desert region of western South America, where it seldom rains from one year's end to the other. There are probably not a dozen umbrellas in all these houses below us, and none of the people need waterproofs or rubber shoes. The people can always depend on dry weather.

The houses of Lima are constructed of mud, because this is the cheapest of building materials. The city, notwithstanding, has a substantial appearance. It seems at first to be made of brick and stone. The mud walls of some of its buildings look like marble; others are painted to imitate granite, and others of bright colors seem to be made of brick covered with plaster. Most of them are in reality nothing but mud, being made of sun-dried brick.

We are surprised at the extent of some of the houses. They are very large. They are usually of one or two stories. In the two-story buildings only the first story is made of sun-dried brick, the second being a combination of mud and bamboo canes.

From the roof we can see the shape of the houses. Each is constructed in the form of a hollow square, with a little court or garden in the center. About the court the people sit at night, this being their favorite lounging place. Many of the windows open on the courts, but much of the light comes from the roofs. Little dormer windows are built up for this purpose from nearly every one of the houses. The dormers look like chicken coops, and it is indeed hard to tell which are the roof windows and which are the real chicken coops.

Yes, I mean chicken coops which contain chickens.

"From the roof we can see the shape of the houses."

Don't you see the coops on the roofs all about us? On that building just over the way the hens are putting their heads out through the slats, and just beyond is a coop in which a rooster is crowing. Thousands of chickens are raised on the tops of the houses of Lima. Chickens are hatched, grow up, and themselves lay eggs, and are finally killed for the kitchens below. It is said, indeed, that some people in Lima keep cows and goats on their roofs, but there are none in sight from where we now stand.

But let us go down and take a walk through the city. The streets are narrow. They cross one another at right angles, with parks or plazas cut out here and there. The

"Each house has a little court in the center."

business streets have awnings out over the sidewalks, and there are many balconies or porches which jut out, so that we are protected from the rays of the sun. It is but a few steps from our hotel to the chief plaza or square, on one side of which is the great Lima cathedral.

This building is one of the finest churches on the South American continent. It is older than any church in our country, and although it is made of sun-dried brick, it has cost millions of dollars. We enter it and take a look at the skeleton of the treacherous Pizarro, which is preserved here in a coffin of glass, and then go out and cross to the opposite side of the square, where is the capitol of Peru.

The country is a republic, and it is in this long, low, two-story building that Congress sits and the president has his offices. There are soldiers at all the entrances, and we see that the ruler of Peru is far more carefully guarded than our president. Elections are not so fair here as in the United States, and when one party is defeated it often brings about a revolution. The soldiers of the defeated party attempt to drive out the president, and if they can do so they take charge of the government until another election is held.

But suppose we go shopping. It is now about four in the afternoon, and for the next hour

"The business streets have awnings."

the streets will be filled with well-dressed people, some chatting together, and others going from store to store buying goods.

The business hours of South American cities are from seven in the morning until eleven, and from one until six in the afternoon. Between eleven and one most of the stores are closed. The merchants go to their breakfasts; for the people like to rest during the heat of the day.

Lima has many fine stores. They have no windows, but the doors are so made that the fronts can be opened, and as we walk through the streets we seem to be passing through a museum with goods of all kinds piled upon the floors.

What queerly dressed women we meet everywhere! They are clad in black, and they look more like nuns than like our own mothers and sisters out walking or shopping at home. Peruvian women do not wear bonnets. Instead, they have fine black cloths draped about their heads and pinned fast at the back of the neck, so that only the face shows. This is the dress the ladies wear on the streets. It is contrary to custom for a woman to go into church with anything else on her head, and if one should attempt to enter wearing a bonnet she would be touched with a stick by the sexton and told to uncover her head. The women of the upper classes when at home dress much as we do, and are quite as fond of gay clothes.

The men wear clothes similar to ours. They have on tall hats and kid gloves, and nearly every one carries a cane. See how they lift their hats, smile, and shake hands when they meet, and how they smile and tip their hats when they part. The Peruvians are very polite, and especially cordial to strangers. One of them will walk a block to show us our way, and if we admire anything he has he will at once offer it to us as a gift. We must not accept such gifts, however, for they are made merely as a matter of form.

During a recent trip in South America I was offered all sorts of things, from diamond rings to poodle dogs and fast horses. One day a rich Peruvian told me that his palace was mine. I felt quite rich for a moment, but when I remembered that the palace was worth a fortune, I knew he could not be in earnest, and politely refused.

But let us leave the stores and walk through the city. The streets are so narrow that the carriages which go this way and that have trouble in passing, and we are often crowded against the walls by the hucksters and milk-women, who ride quite close to the sidewalk to keep out of the throng. The hucksters carry their vegetables about in panniers slung upon donkeys, and the bread man rides a horse with a bag of loaves on each side.

That woman who is coming toward us is a milkwoman. See how she bobs up and down as her pony trots onward. She has her cans in those leather buckets fastened to the sides of the pony, and she is sitting almost on top of the buckets, with her feet about his neck. She is dressed in bright calico and wears above her brown face a broad-brimmed Panama hat. Now she stops and slides

"That is a milkwoman."

down over the horse's neck to the street. She ties a rope around his front legs at the ankles to keep him from running away, and takes one of the buckets into that house.

All the milk of Lima is thus served. The streets are too narrow for carts or large wagons, and the huckstering is done on horses, donkeys, or mules.

Next morning we go to the market. Here we find dozens of donkeys loaded with all sorts of things. We see scores of milkwomen starting out on their horses to peddle milk through the city. The big market house is thronged with cooks and other women buying things for their tables.

As we go by the stalls we see that Peru is a land of good things to eat. There are string beans as long as your arm. They are tied up in bunches and hung upon poles. We see potatoes of all kinds, some of which are as yellow as gold. They are the famous *papas amarillas*, the yellow potatoes of Peru. They are delicious when cooked.

We see sweet potatoes of many varieties, and quantities of yucca, a rootlike tuber somewhat like the potato, used in many of the South American countries. It grows as big around as a baseball bat, and is often two feet in length. It is very white, and its flesh is somewhat waxy and jellylike.

There are roasting ears at almost all the vegetable stands, and squashes, pumpkins, and many kinds of melons. There are oranges, lemons, and alligator pears. There are guavas and pomegranates, pineapples and bananas, peaches and pears, and grapes of many kinds. There are excellent fish, one kind of which is dressed with lemon juice and eaten raw. There are all sorts of meats, and you can buy a kid or a half-dozen guinea pigs for a trifle. The Peruvians are very fond of guinea pigs, and raise them for food. The meat tastes like young pigeon or the tenderest squirrel. We try it ourselves in the form of a stew, and find it delicious.

VIII. UP THE ANDES.

GET out your overcoats, put on your high boots or thick shoes, and take your gloves with you. We are bound for the top of the Andes, and may have to tramp through the snow.

We shall go there upon the Oro'ya Railroad, the steepest railroad of the world. It begins at Callao, on the Pacific, and passes through Lima on its way up the Andes. It was planned by an American named Meiggs, who intended that it should connect the seaport with the famous silver mines of Cerro de Pasco. It would cost so much, however, that it has not been completed. It now extends to a short distance on the other side of the mountains, although it is planned to build it at some time to the navigable tributaries of the Amazon, about three hundred miles farther on.

As it is, the road is less than one hundred and fifty miles long. It is so steep, however, that it will carry us more than three miles above where we now are, and bring us to the great plateau between the tops of the Andes.

Leaving Lima at seven o'clock in the morning, we first travel through the sugar and cotton plantations of the Rimac valley. The fields are as green as Georgia in June. The cotton plants are in blossom, and the plantations look like vast gardens of pink and light-yellow roses. There are gangs of Indian peons, clad in white cotton, working among them. The fields are as well kept as our gardens at home.

We pass several villages of one-story houses, go by a cotton mill and a large sugar factory, and then shoot out of the green into the dry foothills of the Andes. What a change! The vegetation has disappeared. The low hills are bleak and bare in the light of the early morning. We ride for miles, climbing higher and higher, and seeing nothing but dazzling gray rock.

Farther on a thin fuzz of green crops out of the gray. Now a little cactus and small bunches of weeds appear.

Fruit Sellers at Railroad Station.

As we rise higher still the mountains grow greener. At a mile above the sea there is a thin coat of grass, and at two miles we count forty different kinds of flowers at a stopping of the train. There are buttercups without number, and flowers of all colors, the names of which we do not know. It is now winter in the Andes, when halfway up the western slope there are frequent mists or light rains. In summer all is as gray and sterile as the desert below.

Now we are still higher. We have come to a region where only bits of soil are to be seen here and there. Notice how the people till every foot of good ground. The fields on this hill are not bigger than a bedspread, and those on the other side of the valley opposite the railroad seem in the distance the size of a handkerchief. See those green ledges one above the other on the mountainside. They rise almost to the tops of the hills, and were so made that a man could stand on any of the lower ones and weed the crop on the ledge just above. Those terraces were built by the Indians in the time of the Incas. They are used only for grazing to-day.

Now we have stopped at a station. About it there is a village of huts with walls of sun-dried brick and roofs of gray thatch. The stones upon the roof have been laid there to keep the strong winds from lifting the thatch. How small the huts are, and how mean! Some are not better than dog kennels. They are the homes of the people who are gathering about us as we stand on the platform. They are dark-faced Indian men, women, and children, dressed in white cottons. You may see more of them at work in the fields, or tending the sheep which graze in the mountains.

How pure the air is, and how grand the scenes all about us! The mountains rise almost straight up over our heads. The railroad hangs to their sides, and we ride for miles between walls of rock which look like gigantic cathedrals, their spires lost in the clouds. We shoot through tunnels which wind about like the letter S, and cross steel bridges over deep canyons above mountain streams. Every turn brings new pictures, some of which are of terrible grandeur.

What a triumph of modern engineering was the building of this track up the Andes! It cost many millions of dollars and thousands of lives. The road goes up some of the steepest mountains of the globe. Much of its bed was cut out of the rocks. At times the men had to be lowered in baskets over the precipices to drill holes for the

"We shoot through tunnels."

blasting. The tracks wind this way and that, one above the other, so that in places we can count five different tracks which run parallel one over the other, showing us how the road had to zigzag to climb its way up.

Farther up the air grows colder. At two miles we pass through a rainstorm, and later on are surrounded by snow. Now the mist and clouds have come down about us, and we are enveloped in fog. A little higher, and we are above the clouds. There the wind is carrying the clouds down the Andes, the air becomes clear, and we shudder at the precipices along which the track crawls.

Now we are on the tops of the Andes. That white peak above us is Mount Meiggs. Its summit is more than seventeen thousand feet above the sea, and where we stop at the entrance to the Galera tunnel, going through the mountain, we are three miles higher up in the air than when we started this morning.

We are on the highest railroad point in the world, far above the height of Fujiyama, the sacred snow capped mountain of Japan. We are about as high up as Mont Blanc or any point in Europe, and a thousand feet higher than Pikes Peak or any other mountain in the United States outside Alaska. There is a blue glacier hanging over us on the top of Mount Meiggs, and right under it, in the middle of the tunnel, is a place where the waters flowing to the Atlantic and Pacific divide. We go in and take a drink from the stream at the side of the railroad, which is trickling on its way to the Rimac river and the Pacific, and then by a jump reach a place where we bend over and scoop up some water which is about starting down the east slope of the Andes into one of the tributaries of the Amazon, on its way to the Atlantic.

We walk farther on through the tunnel to the eastern slope of the Andes. There are snow banks outside at the edge of the tunnel, and we start a snow fight away up here in the clouds. We are soon glad to stop. The air is so rare that every throw sends our hearts into our throats, and we pant for breath. We try to yell, but our voices are weak from the thinness of the air, and the yell ends in a squeak. Our boots grow suddenly heavy. We walk slowly, and in climbing the hills we crawl. Some of us are attacked with the mountain sickness, which comes to

Entrance to the Galera Tunnel.

many when they first go so high up in the air. We have terrible headaches, and at the same time feel severe nausea.

During our first night in the mountains we cannot sleep. Some of us faint away, and blood flows from our mouths, eyes, and noses. The sickness soon passes off, however, and we then enjoy the strange sights and pure air of the Andes.

IX. ON THE ROOF OF SOUTH AMERICA.

WE start southward this morning upon the high plateau of the Andes. The cold air bites our noses. There are snowy mountains on each side of us. We are on what might be called the roof of the South American continent. The Andes are among the highest mountains of the globe. They have several peaks which rise more than four miles above the sea. We saw some of the greatest of them in Ecuador, and we shall travel among others on our way south through Peru and Bolivia.

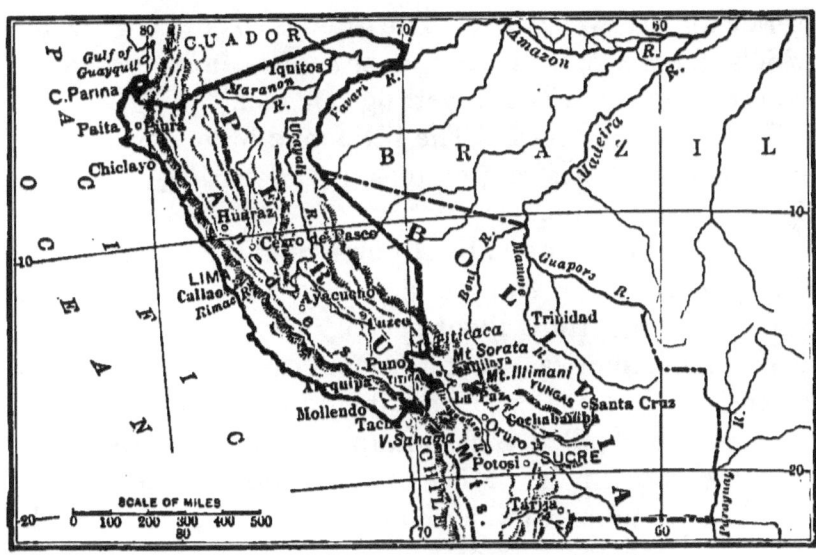

Peru and Bolivia.

The highest of the Andes is Mount Aconcagua (ä-cŏn-cä′guä), in Chile. It is 23,910 feet high. Beginning with it and running northward to Ecuador, the mountains extend in an irregular double chain, upholding this lofty plateau upon which we now are. The plateau in some parts of Peru is five hundred miles wide, and much of it is about two miles and a half above the sea.

We are many days riding on horseback upon it to Bolivia. Now and then we make excursions into the hills, to the camps where men are mining for silver and gold. The Andes of this region are noted for their mineral deposits, and great quantities of the precious metals are taken out of them every year.

We spend the most of the time, however, upon the plateau. We ride on and on over a desolate plain covered with a scanty growth of fuzzy green grass. How it rains! This is the winter season. We have a storm of hail, snow, or rain almost every day. The grass is soaked with water, which it holds like a sponge, and we cannot get down from our horses without wetting our feet.

There are few trees. The little mud huts which we see have small patches of potatoes, green barley, or quinua (keen'wa) about them.

This plateau is the natural home of the potato. It was taken from here to Europe, and is said to have been first introduced into Italy about seventy years after Columbus discovered America. Later on potatoes were cultivated extensively in Ireland, so many being used there that they are sometimes called Irish potatoes. The potatoes we see here are very small. Most of them are not bigger than walnuts. It takes a milder climate and richer soil to make them grow to the size of the large potatoes sold in our markets.

We are so high up that barley will not ripen. That which we see is grown for forage. The quinua, to a certain extent, takes the place of other grains in these highlands. It is a plant which looks much like dockweed. It has yellow or red leaves, and its seeds when shelled out are white. They are like hominy ground fine. Quinua is eaten as mush and is cooked in stews.

There are also dandelions and other hardy flowers on the plains, and there are many evergreen bushes, which grow only as tall as our ankles, for all things are stunted here away up in the air.

What are those queer animals we see in the pastures? We now and then meet droves of them going along with bags on their backs. They are bigger than sheep, but they look not unlike them, for they are covered with wool. They have long necks, with heads like a camel's. Their

Llamas.

feet and legs are like those of a deer. See how gracefully they walk. Notice how they hold their little heads in the air, pricking up their ears as they see us, for all the world like so many Skye terriers. Those are llamas, the odd little animals which act as beasts of burden upon this highland.

Are they not beautiful? Some are snow white, some seal brown, and a few black and spotted. Their wool is long. It is used by the Indians to make ponchos, blankets, and clothes.

Let us examine the llamas more closely. Take this drove which is coming toward us, each little animal carrying a bag of silver ore on his back. Notice how small the loads are. Each load weighs just one hundred pounds. The llama is very particular as to how much he does, and that is the biggest load he will stand. If you put on more he will not cry or groan, as the camel does, but will calmly kneel down and not move until his load is made right.

Look out! Don't stroke that beast over there! Don't you see he is angry by the way he is shaking his head?

And do llamas bite?

They do not bite, but when they are angry they spit, and I would rather have three camels bite me than be spat upon by one llama. A llama's spittle has the most offensive of smells. The little beast chews its cud like a cow. It has a special place somewhere in its body which is well filled with fluid for such an occasion. If once hit you will find it hard to get the stench out of your clothes, and you cannot go on with our party until you have had a bath and a change. Most of the llamas, however, are gentle, and we fall in love with them as we see them everywhere on the plains.

But are these little llamas on the pastures through which we are riding? Some are black, and some are snow white. No; those are not llamas, although they look like them. They are alpacas, a domestic animal which is valued for its long, silky wool. The wool is straighter and stronger than sheep's wool. It is used for shawls, fine clothes, and umbrellas, and much of it goes from Peru to our country.

The vicuña (ve-coon'ya) is an animal of much the same species, which runs wild in these regions. We may have a chance to shoot one later on. It runs like a deer and is very wary. Vicuña fur is like yellow velvet, and we can buy rugs of it in the stores of the Bolivian cities. Still farther south we shall see the guanaco, which also looks like the llama. It has yellow-and-white fur about as long as that of a rabbit.

In our journey we now and then cross high valleys which cut through the plateau. Here the climate is milder, and we find all kinds of semitropical fruits.

In one of these valleys Cuzco (koos'kō), the capital of the Incas, was located.

Vicuña.

The town was situated at a place where three rivers meet, at more than two miles above the sea. There is a small city standing on the same site to-day. We see here the ruins of the great temples which the Spaniards found in the days of Pizarro. Then Cuzco was the chief city of the great nation of civilized Indians which inhabited almost the whole of western South America. It was a grand city, and some of its temples were plated with gold. The Spaniards tore seven hundred gold plates, each as big as the lid of a large chest, from the walls of the Temple of the Sun, and when they left after their first visit their horses were loaded with gold.

At that time the plateau was quite thickly populated. It is still so to-day. Cuzco itself has about twenty thousand inhabitants, and most of the people of Peru live in these plains between the two ranges of mountains.

We are surprised to see so many Indians. In Cuzco there are twelve Indians to one white man, and on our way down the plateau we meet many queer-looking Indian men, women, and children. They are in their bare feet, and they wear an odd dress.

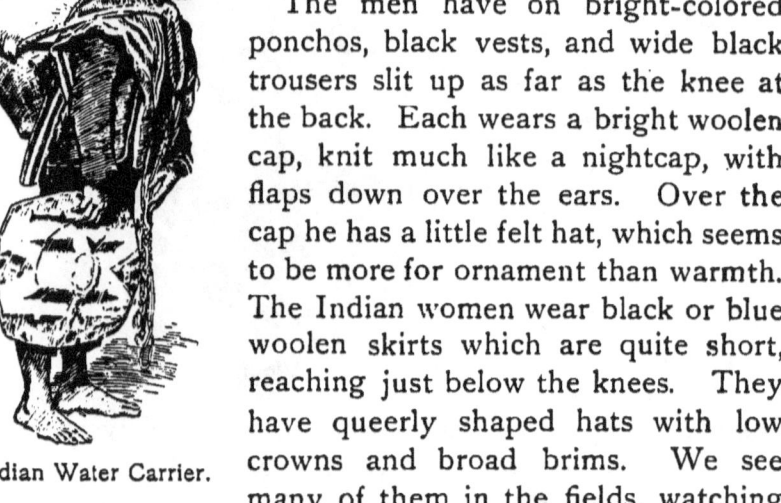

Indian Water Carrier.

The men have on bright-colored ponchos, black vests, and wide black trousers slit up as far as the knee at the back. Each wears a bright woolen cap, knit much like a nightcap, with flaps down over the ears. Over the cap he has a little felt hat, which seems to be more for ornament than warmth. The Indian women wear black or blue woolen skirts which are quite short, reaching just below the knees. They have queerly shaped hats with low crowns and broad brims. We see many of them in the fields, watching the llamas, alpacas, and sheep. They are very industrious. Each has a long spool of wool in her hand, and she spins llama wool as she watches her flock.

We meet more Indians as we go on toward Lake Titicaca, and we shall see their mud villages everywhere during our journeys on the high plateau of Bolivia. They belong to the two tribes, the Quichua (ke-choo'ä) and Aymara (i-mä-rä'), the same tribes which were here when the Spaniards first came. Even now they number more than a million.

They are queer people, and have habits and ways of

their own. Most of them are little more than slaves to the white and mixed races who own the most of the lands. Each farm has a little colony of Indians upon it, and each Indian family has its mud hut. Throughout the whole year the Indians work three days each week for the

"Each Indian family has its mud hut."

owner of the land, as rent for their little huts and the small patches of ground about them. The remaining three days they have for themselves. If their master does not want their work, he can hire them out to others, and if they do not obey he can punish them.

The Indians are very docile, and will bear much without getting angry. It is said they love their masters and will band together to fight for them. The Indians of the different farms often have quarrels, and at such times each band marches upon the other as though in actual warfare. They sometimes use guns, but more often slings, with which they throw stones with great force and skill, sometimes killing one another in their fights.

Let us enter an Indian hut. The one we select would hardly make a respectable pigsty for one of our farms. It is of mud, and is not more than ten feet square. Its thatched roof is so low that we can touch it when we stand outside the front door, and as we go in we have to stoop down, besides lifting our feet up as high as a chair to get over the mud sill and through the hole which serves as an entrance. Inside there is only about enough space in which to turn round. One side of the room is filled with farm tools. On the other side is a donkey, and the chickens squawk as they run here and there to get out of our way. There is little furniture. The people sit on the floor. They often sleep sitting, huddling themselves close together for warmth.

Indian with Sling.

That little clay pot over there with the ashes beneath it is the stove. The hut has no chimney, and the smoke finds its way out as it can. The cooking is simple. A favorite dish is challona stew, with chuño (choon'yō), or frozen potatoes, mixed with it. Challona is dried mutton. The sheep is split open when killed, and then left out to freeze. When it is stiff, water is sprinkled over it, and it is frozen again. It is then hung up and dried, after which it becomes so tough that it will keep for months. It must, however, be cut up in small bits and boiled a long time before it is tender; then the natives think it is delicious.

We find chuño for sale in the markets of Cuzco, and we can buy it everywhere on the high plateau of the Andes. It looks like bits of bleached bones, or perhaps more like the large flat pebbles you find on the seashore. It is really potatoes which are frozen and dried, so that they can be kept for a year without spoiling. The raw potatoes are first soaked in water, being wet every day, and left out at night until they freeze. Next the skins are trodden off with the bare feet, and the potatoes are thoroughly dried in the air. They are now as white as snow and as hard as rock. They are soaked before cooking, and are usually served as a stew. We eat some, but they are rather insipid.

X. STEAMBOATING ABOVE THE CLOUDS.

STEAMBOATING above the clouds! Floating over some of the highest waters of the globe! Sailing in sight of glacial snows amid the tops of the Andes, so near the sky that heaven and earth seem to meet close around us, and make us think we are on the very roof of the world! We are outside the harbor of Puno (poo′no), on the broad waters of Lake Titicaca.

The air is so clear we can see for miles. That blue mass in front is Titicaca Island. It will take us four hours to steam to it, but it looks quite near as it lies there like a great blue balloon on the water. There are other masses of blue here and there. There are altogether eight large islands in the lake, some of which are inhabited. Now we are steaming by one. See, the bits of land between the rocks are green with scanty crops of potatoes, barley, and quinua. The soil is cultivated to the tops of

Indians in Balsas, Lake Titicaca.

the hills, and red-faced Indians are at work in the fields. Their huts of stone and thatch are down near the shore. Some have llamas, sheep, and donkeys tethered about them.

How grand are the mountains! There is nothing finer in the Himalayas or the Alps than the snowy peaks which rise above us. That silvery mass to the north is Sorata (so-rä′tä), next to Aconcagua the highest of the Andes. The great wall of mountains which stretches from it south there to the east is the Sorata range, and that tall peak rising high over the others is Illimani (ēl-yē-mä′nē), which is about four miles in height.

This lake upon which we are floating is higher up in the air than most of the mountain tops in our country. Is it not a wonderful body of water? It is almost half as large as Lake Ontario, and it lies here twice as high as the top of Mount Washington. Those little huts we see on the islands are among the highest houses in the world in which people live, and this is really the loftiest of all lakes upon which steamboats sail.

But where does the lake come from, and where does it go? We can easily see its source by looking at the snows and glaciers about us. It is made by the snow water of nine rivers from the Andean peaks, which flow into it. Where the water all goes is not known. The lake remains at about the same level from one year's end to the other, although it has no visible outlet to the sea. A part of its waters go into the river Desaguadero (dās-ä-gwä-dā′rō) and on into a lake of the same name, or, as it is called in Bolivia, Lake Poo′po. Lake Poopo has no outlet that can be seen.

But let us take a look at our ship. It is carrying us over Lake Titicaca at twelve miles an hour. It is as beautiful as a gentleman's yacht. It is named the *Choya*, and when we look at the engine we find there is a plate stating that the ship was built away off in Glasgow, Scotland.

This seems very strange. How could they possibly get such a big ship over the Andes? The *Choya* weighs so much that if it could be loaded on wagons a thousand horses could not pull it. How could they possibly lift such a weight over these mountains, which everywhere in Peru are almost as high as Pikes Peak?

Of course they could not if they tried to lift the ship all at once. But such a vessel was needed for commerce, and commerce works in all sorts of ways to secure its own ends. All of its parts were put on a steamer and brought from Glasgow around through the Strait of Magellan to the seaport Mollendo, in southern Peru.

"Let us take a look at our ship."

At Mollendo there is the beginning of a railroad quite as wonderful as that upon which we came over the Andes from Lima. It is three hundred miles long, and connects the seacoast with Arequipa (ä-rä-kē′pä), one of the chief cities of Peru, and also with Puno, on Lake Titicaca. The parts of the ship were put on the car at Mollendo, and the engines puffed as they carried them over the Andes.

At Puno they were taken off, joined together, and launched on the lake, so that to-day we can sail upon these high waters in a floating house made in Scotland. This is one of the wonders of commerce.

We are still more interested when the engineer tells us that the coal he is using comes from Australia, so that both sides of the world seem to be working to help us along on our journey.

When we examine the freight on the *Choya* we see how the ship has become one of the agents of commerce. We have goods from different parts of the world which we are carrying to Bolivia, and the captain tells us that he is to bring back a load of copper, gold, silver, tin, and Peruvian bark, to be sent from Puno down to the Pacific. Who knows but that some of that copper will be used in the same works in Glasgow where the steamer was made, and whether some of the silver and gold may not find its way to Australia to pay the very miners who have furnished our coal?

Now we are approaching Chililaya (chē-lǐ-lä′yä), the port of Bolivia. We see many boats near the shore. Some are starting out to bring freight to the steamer. What queer things they are! They appear to be made of straw, but men are working upon them, and there is one that has a donkey and a llama on board. Some have straw sails, and others are being poled through the water. Those boats are bal′sas, a curious craft used by the Indians of Lake Titicaca. They are just like the boats which the Spaniards found these people using centuries ago.

There is one which has come close to our steamer. It is made of long reeds, which grow in quantities on the edge of the lake. The reeds are laid together and tied tightly in rolls. They are so woven and fastened that they form a raftlike boat which will float on the water.

But we have at last reached the wharf. There is a crowd of Indians ready to unload the steamer. We hand over our baggage to two queer-looking fellows, and walk with them to the shore. Here there are hundreds of

Inca Ruins, Lake Titicaca.

mules with goods awaiting shipment to Puno. There are droves of llamas which have brought in packages of rubber and coffee, and there are numerous donkeys carrying the bark from which quinine is made. We stop a moment, watching the drivers unload their beasts, and then walk on up the hill to the rude little hotel where we have to stay overnight.

XI. TRAVELS IN BOLIVIA.

WHEN we land at Chililaya we are in Bolivia. We are just forty-seven miles from its chief city, La Paz. We take a stage drawn by eight mules for the journey. We go on the gallop all day long, stopping only to change mules every three hours. We sit outside with the driver. He is an Indian. He has a little pile of stones beside him, from which he now and then makes a good throw at the long ears of such of the animals as are lagging behind.

The ride is delightful. The air is always bracing on the high plateau of Bolivia. It is so clear we can see for miles. To the east is a great wall of snow mountains, with Illimani rising above the rest of the peaks, and away off to the west are lower hills, which seem to climb over one another and finally end in snow at the sky. Now we pass a mud hut, and now a flock of llamas, alpacas, or sheep, feeding on the thin grass; but other than this there is nothing about us but the sky, the plains, and the mountains.

As we near the close of the day we look for the city to which we are going. We are hungry, and wonder whether we shall get there before dark, when at last the driver pulls up the mules on their haunches, and the stage stops. We are on the brink of a precipice, and there a thousand feet below us, in a little gorge in the mountains, is the curious city of La Paz.

It is so far down that we can hardly distinguish the houses. They look like a jumble of bright-colored boxes, with trees here and there rising out above their red roofs. They grow plainer as we gallop on our winding way down the steep slopes of the hill. We are soon riding between walled gardens, and at last the stage stops in the heart of the town.

How queer it all is! Most of the people about us are clad in the brightest of reds, blues, and greens. Every other man wears a poncho, or blanket, with his head

La Paz, Bolivia.

through a hole in its center, and some of the women have striped shawls, bright-colored short skirts, and queerly shaped hats. Five eighths of the people are Indians, and the remainder are whites and of the mixed race of Indians and whites called cho'los.

Even the houses are a blaze of bright colors. Their walls are painted in the most delicate tints of red, blue, and green. There is a lavender grocery store; next to it a shoe shop of rose pink; and farther on are other establishments of cream and sky blue. The houses are of one or two stories. The shops are open to the street, so that we can see all that goes on within.

But where can we get a cab or dray to carry our baggage to the hotel? There are none in sight, and we learn there are none in La Paz. The streets are so narrow and so up hill and down that no vehicles are used in the city, and all freighting is done by donkeys, ponies, llamas, and men. The Indian porters will carry our boxes. There are a dozen porters about the stage office. We give each man a trunk, and he trots off to the hotel up the hills with the trunk on his back, while we walk behind.

The next morning we start out for a tour of the city, going up the hills very slowly, for the air is so pure that we are soon out of breath.

We visit the markets. It is early morning, but the streets are filled with buyers and sellers, with Indians, cholos, and whites, dressed in all colors of the rainbow.

Cholo Girl.

There are scores of Indian women carrying fruit and vegetables to the markets for sale. Their burdens are tied up in striped blankets of blue, red, yellow, and green, and they bend half double as they walk onward. They squat down on the streets and spread their wares out before them, peddling them by the piece or the pile.

There are Indian men wearing bright ponchos, and such a lot of Indian babies that we have to pick our way carefully to keep from treading upon them. Some lie on the cold stones and play with the merchandise their mothers are selling. Some are too young to crawl, and their big eyes peep out of the shawls in which they are tied to the backs of their mothers. Most of the babies are laughing. There is one crying, and over there is another which has crawled away from its mother and is almost under the feet of those llamas which are coming up the street. Now its mother sees it and runs to save it.

"The Indian porters carry our boxes."

Stop and look at the queer things for sale all about us. What funny potatoes! Those in that pile are not bigger than chestnuts, and they are as pink as the toes of the baby who is playing among them. There are some of a violet color, while those in the next pile are as black as your boots. The white ones beside that woman over the way are chuno, and have been frozen for sale.

What a variety of fruits! We find some on every corner, and the market is filled with quinces, peaches, and pears, as well as oranges, lemons, and pineapples. The fruit all comes from the lands lower down, for it is only a few days' ride on muleback from here to the tropical valleys of the Andes, and there are all kinds of climates farther down the mountains, and all kinds of fruits.

Bolivian Boys.

What are those big green bean pods that woman is selling? They are not beans at all. They are a kind of fruit which is eaten raw. If you will buy one and break it open you will see that the seeds within it are imbedded in a pulp which looks like spun silk. We smack our lips as we eat it, for when it is cold it is very much like finely flavored ice cream.

Is this not a wonderful country where all kinds of fruits grow so near together? Yes, indeed; Bolivia is naturally one of the rich countries of the world. In the eastern part of it, below the plateau, there are great plains upon which vast herds of cattle are feeding. In its forests there are rubber trees, from which the sap is gathered and shipped down the Beni and Madeira to the mouth of the Amazon, whence it is sent all over the world to be used for making tires, coats, overshoes, and all sorts of such things. There are parts of Bolivia that have never been explored, and we could easily ride down the eastern slopes of the mountains and come into a region inhabited only by the most savage of Indians.

Some of the wild Indians are cannibals. Some go about naked, and some wear plates of wood and metal in the lobes of their ears, each plate being as large as a silver dollar. Many of them make war upon white men, and some use blowguns, with which they shoot poisoned arrows at their enemies. The guns are reeds from ten to twelve feet long, and the slightest scratch of one of the arrows causes immediate death.

On the eastern slopes of the Andes, by a very short ride on muleback, we could reach the Yungas valley, where there are plantations of coffee, coca, and cinchona trees.

Have you ever heard of cinchona?

Perhaps not, but I venture every one of you has sometime had to take quinine. Quinine is the bitter white powder made from the bark of the cinchona tree. It is especially good for malarial fevers, and we shall need some later on when we go up the Amazon.

Cinchona

We see loads of cinchona bark on the streets of La Paz. That little donkey which is just turning the corner has a bundle of it on each side of his back. Other donkeys are coming behind him, each of which carries a load. That drove is bringing the bark into La Paz. Here it will be repacked and shipped to all parts of the world.

Let us go and pull out a piece of the bark and take a bite of it. How bitter it is! It tastes like quinine.

Bolivia raises some of the best cinchona, although excellent cinchona is also raised in Peru and all along the eastern slopes of the Andes between here and Colombia.

Plantations have been recently started for raising cinchona trees. Six years after planting, the trees are cut down and their bark stripped off for quinine. At this age each tree will produce about four pounds of bark. The next year after cutting, sprouts will come up from the stumps, and six years later another crop is ready for harvest.

The most of the quinine of commerce, however, comes from wild trees. The bark we tasted on the streets of La Paz was gathered from the forests at the head of the Beni river. It was carried through the woods for miles on the backs of Indians, and was then loaded upon the donkeys which brought it to La Paz.

But what is that we see on those other donkeys which are now going by us? The bundles are of about the same size as the cinchona bundles, but the stuff within them looks like leaves. That is coca leaves, from which cocaine, a drug used to deaden pain, is made. Dentists often put cocaine in a sensitive tooth when it has to be filled.

Coca is also used by the Indians on the Bolivian plateau as a chew. Every Indian we meet has a lump of coca inside his cheek, and men, women, and children are chewing it all day long. The Indians in the mines will not work unless their employers give them, in addition to their wages, some coca to chew every day, and all of the Indians would rather have coca than coffee, tea, or tobacco.

Vast quantities of it are produced every year, and are shipped on llamas and donkeys to all parts of Bolivia, to Peru, and to Chile.

You must not confound coca with chocolate, or cacao, which is sometimes called cocoa, nor with the cocoanut tree. The coca plant is a shrub which grows from four to

The Alamada or Promenade, La Paz.

six feet in height. It has leaves much like our wintergreen shrub. They are very stimulating, and the Indians tell us that chewing coca will keep out the cold and also satisfy hunger.

We try a chew ourselves, putting some lime with it as the Indians do. The leaves taste rather bitter, the lime burns our tongues, and as the habit seems very disgusting, we decide to leave coca alone.

XII. THE MINERAL WEALTH OF THE ANDES.

AT La Paz we are not far from some of the richest mining regions of the world. The lofty Andes throughout their whole length, from the Isthmus of Panama to the Strait of Magellan, contain some gold. The Sorata range, which now looks down upon us, has rich veins of tin, and vast quantities of copper are yearly taken out of the mountains to the north and to the south.

There is so much gold on the east slope of the Peruvian Andes that during the floods the streams wash down grains and nuggets of gold. Many of the streams are dry part of the year, and the Indians have paved them with stones, so that the heavy gold is caught in the cracks when it drops. The golden grains are thus carried down when the rivers are high, and so caught

Hydraulic Mining.

that they can be picked up when the streams fall. This was one of the gold-mining methods of the Incas, and it was thus that much of the gold which the Spaniards took from them was gathered.

We see men washing gold in many places as we ride through Bolivia. The miners are Indians employed by the white men. There are some at work near La Paz. They take the gravel and dirt to the sides of the streams, and roll it about in wooden bowls as big as those in which we knead bread. From time to time they dip up a little water into the bowl, and shake it around so that all the dirt melts into the water and can be poured out.

Washing Gold.

After a while there is nothing but the gold and the gravel. The miners throw the gravel away handful by handful, first looking it carefully over and dropping back into the bowl the little yellow bits which they see. Finally all the gravel has been thrown out, and there is left a little pile of yellow pebbles and grains, some of which are not bigger than the end of a needle. This is the gold. Such methods of mining are wasteful, for much of the gold dust is so small that the grains cannot be seen. It is only lately that mercury and other modern means which we employ to collect gold have been much used.

When we visit the silver mines, we find that most of the work there is done with rude tools. In the older mines the Indians use hammers and drills to break up the ore. They carry it out of the mines on their backs in sacks of rawhide.

Silver is found in veins of ore in the rocks, and these veins often extend far down under the earth. Some of the mines are hence very deep. The Indians climb out of them upon ladders or notched sticks, with heavy sacks of ore on their backs. They work almost naked, wearing only breechcloths about their waists, singing weird songs as they dig out the ore.

After the ore is taken from the mines it is broken up into small pieces with hammers by women and children. The best of it is then ground to powder by rolling great stones over it. The powder is mixed with mercury, which dissolves the silver out of the dust, and by other chemical processes it is then made ready for the use of man.

Some of the richest silver mines of the world are in the Andes. A little north of Mount Meiggs, where we crossed the coast range in Peru, is the town of Cerro de Pasco, built about one of the richest bodies of silver ore ever known. This body was about a mile long and more than half a mile wide.

The mine was discovered several hundred years ago, in a curious way. An Indian shepherd had wandered to this place one day with his flock. He found the air very cold as evening drew on, and kindled a fire, before which he lay down to sleep. When he awoke the next morning he discovered that the stone upon which his fire had been built had melted and turned to silver. Since then thousands of tons of pure silver have been taken out of that spot, and many of the llamas we saw on our way to Mount Meiggs loaded with silver had come from Cerro de Pasco.

Bags of Silver.

There are other rich silver regions in different parts of Peru, and in the Bolivian highlands there is a strip of country, wider than the state of Pennsylvania, and as long as the distance from Philadelphia to Omaha, which is dotted with silver mines.

Bolivia has perhaps given more silver to the world than any other country. It has a mountain called Potosi (po-tō'sĭ), out of which has been taken almost three billion dollars' worth of silver—so much that, could it have been melted up and made into teaspoons, it would have furnished enough to have given two solid silver spoons to every man, woman, and child upon the globe.

A ride of three days from La Paz over the plateau brings us to the town of Oruro (ō-roo'rō), a few miles from Lake Poopo. Oruro has twelve thousand people. It lies at the foot of rocky mountains, and it is almost surrounded by mines which contain rich veins of silver and tin.

Tin mines are not so common in the world as mines of silver and gold, but tin is of such a character that a little of it goes a great way. It is largely used as a coating for sheets of iron, to protect them from rust. The tin cups, pans, and pails, and other such things which we use are made of tin plate, which is merely iron plated with tin.

The only mines which gave much tin to the world until within about two hundred years were those of southern England. The mines there are still worked, but Great Britain uses so much tin that this is not nearly enough, and she imports a great deal from far-away lands. It is the same with the other countries of Europe, and also with the United States. Just now a great deal of tin comes from the Strait of Malacca, from different parts of Australia, and from the rich mines which we find in Peru and Bolivia.

We spend some time in the tin mines of Oruro. They

Breaking up Tin Ore.

are noted for the fine quality of their ore. It looks to us much like silver. Much of it does contain silver. We learn that both silver and tin are often found mixed together in the same vein.

The ore is dug from the rocks with hammers and drills. It is broken to pieces and then ground to powder. It is next put into a furnace with other materials, and melted through a process called smelting. After this, when the furnace is opened, all the rock and dirt passes off, and the pure tin flows away in a bright, silverlike stream. It is run into molds, each of which contains fifty pounds. The molds soon cool, forming the bricks of tin which are shipped to all parts of the world.

XIII. ON THE NITRATE DESERT AND THE GUANO ISLANDS.

PUT on your dark spectacles this morning. You will need them to protect your eyes from the sun, for we are about to travel again over the glaring sands of the desert. The country about Oruro is sterile enough, but the lands through which we must pass on our way down to the sea are among the most barren parts of the world.

We take the little narrow gauge railroad, which was built to bring the tin and silver and other things of Lower Bolivia to the sea, and shoot out into vast plains, upon which everything looks gray, bare, and forbidding. Now we cross fields of salt which dazzle our eyes under the glare of the sun, and go into regions of volcanic rock upon which nothing green grows.

We go by two large blue lakes, near the shores of which

are what look like great cakes of ice. Our lips are dry and parched, and we long for a drink. The train stops at a station, and we ask the conductor if some of the ice cannot be brought into the car. The conductor replies that the white stuff is not ice at all. He says it is borax, and that the water of the lake is not fit to drink.

He brings us a lump of borax from a pile which has just arrived at the station to be sent off to Europe. It looks like the finest spun silk wadded up or woven into a lump, and he tells us that it is used in making beads, glass, and cement, and for glazing pottery ware. It is also of value in preserving meat, fish, and milk, and forms a part of some kinds of medicines. It is good for sore eyes, and is very cleansing as a wash for the hair.

The body of water at which we are looking is the great borax lake of Ascotan', out of which thousands of tons of borax are taken each year and shipped to all parts of the world. The borax crystallizes in the waters of the lake, and gathers in a crust on the edges or falls to the bottom. It is produced by certain materials in the volcanic soil about it, or perhaps by vapor which bursts up through the ground from the volcanic mountains which are found in this part of Bolivia.

Is it not odd that such things should come out of the earth? Yes, indeed; but as we go farther down toward the sea we shall enter a region in Chile which is even more strange. There is a part of the coast desert where for hundreds of miles the sands are underlaid with a great bed of nitrate of soda. Nitrate of soda is a salt used for making nitric acid and also for enriching the soil.

We use vast quantities of it in the United States, and more than a million tons are shipped from this desert to Europe every year. It is so valuable indeed that cities have grown up on this barren coast, inhabited by the people who dig out the nitrate of soda and prepare it for sale. Such a town is Antofagasta (än-tō-fä-gäs′tä), where we end our railroad journey from the plateau to the sea. It contains twenty-five thousand people, and is one of the most thriving ports on the Pacific coast of South America.

Making our way through the nitrate fields to the north, we come to a still larger city, Iquique (ĭ-kē′kä), the chief nitrate port of the world.

What a queer place for a town! Iquique is on the edge of the sea, below ragged hills. It is built on the sand. There is not a blade of grass in the country about it. It has not a drop of water from year's end to year's end, except that which is brought to it in ships or in the iron pipe, seventy-five miles long, which connects it with some springs in a desert oasis.

Still, it is a thriving little city. It has stores, schools, newspapers, telephones, electric lights, and street cars. We can buy anything we want in its markets, including the most delicious fruits and the best of fresh meats. Such things are brought in by ships from other parts of the coast, and from nitrate alone comes the money that pays for them all.

The nitrate is found on the east side of a low range of hills from fifteen to ninety miles back from the sea. It is in the form of a rocky stratum with layers of salt rock and sand above it, although sometimes it lies on the top of the ground. It is not known just how it was formed. Some people suppose that the desert was once the bed of an inland sea, and that vast quantities of seaweed, containing nitrogen, having been covered with sand, decayed, and, under the peculiar conditions of this region, became nitrate of soda.

In getting out the nitrate rock a hole about a foot wide is bored down through the sand, salt rock, and nitrate to the soft earth underneath. A small boy is now let down into the hole. He scoops a pocket out of the earth just under the stratum of nitrate, and fills it with powder, inserting a fuse which extends up over the top.

Nitrate Fields.

The boy is then pulled out and the fuse lighted. There is a loud explosion. A cloud of yellow smoke and dust goes up into the air, and the earth for a wide distance about is broken to pieces. The nitrate rock is now dug out with picks and crowbars.

It must be further treated, however, before it is ready for sale. Pure nitrate of soda is not found in nature, and the rock we see thus blown out of the desert is more than half dirt and sand. It is loaded on carts and carried to factories which have been built in the fields.

The factories have great boiling tanks, heated by steam pipes which run through them. Into these tanks of hot water the lumps of nitrate are thrown. The boiling melts up the rock, and just as salt melts and goes into water, so the nitrate salt is taken up by the water of the tank, while the dirt and sand sink to the bottom.

After a time all of the nitrate of soda has gone out of the rock into the boiling water. It now looks for all the world like pale maple sirup.

Diagram of Nitrate Bed.

This fluid is drawn from the boiler and run into cooling tanks. In these the nitrate soon crystallizes and sinks to the bottom, so that after a time each tank is filled with what looks like white sugar, while the water on top has become almost clear. The deposit is nitrate of soda.

The water is now allowed to flow off, and the nitrate is shoveled out into piles to dry in the sun. It is next bagged up in sacks of three hundred pounds each and taken on the railroad to the seacoast, to be shipped to the United States and to Europe.

There is another thing which comes from the nitrate rock which is carefully saved. This is iodine, a crystalline substance which is used in photography and for making dyes and many kinds of valuable drugs. It is obtained from the boiled water out of which the nitrate has been taken. Into the water a certain quantity of bisulphite of soda is put. This causes all the iodine in the water to drop to the bottom in a dirty black powder. This powder is washed, and heated in tight iron boxes. It soon turns to vapor, and is then conducted from the boxes into pipes of fire clay. As the vapor touches the clay it cools and changes to crystals of a beautiful violet color. These crystals are the iodine of commerce. They are shipped to Europe, and thence sent to all parts of the world.

Is it not curious that men should go so far and work so hard merely to get food for the soil? The earth is much like man in that it will not work well—that is, produce good crops for many years in succession—without being fed. The most of the nitrate is used as food for lands which are expected to yield the richest of crops.

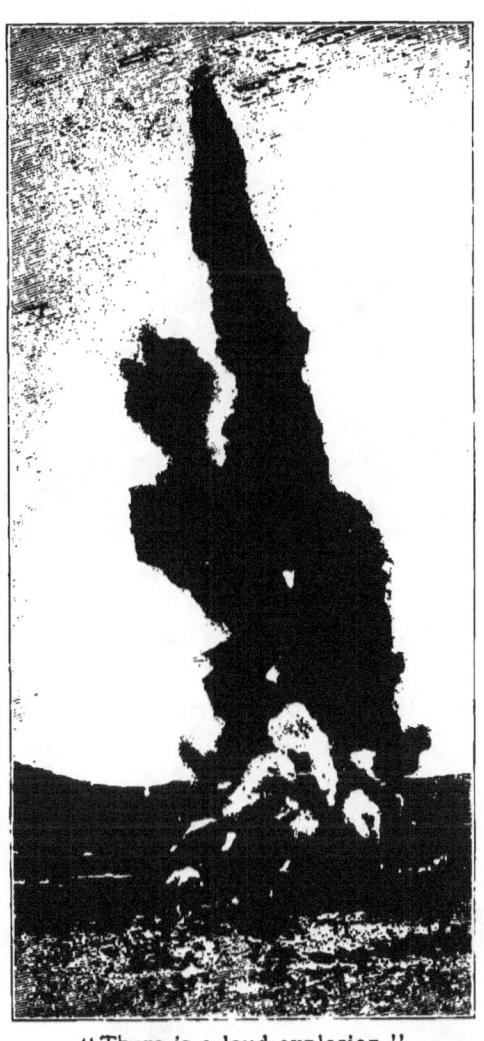

"There is a loud explosion."

Good soil foods are so valuable indeed that farmers

Nitrate Factory.

will pay high prices for them, and vast fortunes have been made out of other such things which are found in this part of South America.

Next to nitrate of soda the chief of these is guano. Guano is a mixture of the manure of birds, dead seals, and fish, which is found along certain parts of the seacoast and on a number of islands not far from the shores of Peru and Chile. The islands are volcanic rocks. They are as bare as the desert. They have not a blade of grass or any green thing upon them, and are merely rock masses covered with what looks much like sand.

If you stir this sand up it will give forth a smell like ammonia, and if you put it upon the soil it will cause it to produce bountiful crops. If we should stay on the islands overnight we could see that they are then covered by the birds which have for ages chosen them as their roosting places and homes. They are the pelicans and sea gulls which feed by the millions in the waters of this part of the Pacific. They often bring the fish they have caught in their bills to the islands and leave them there. During some parts of the year, many seals come here to breed, and seals often crawl out of the sea upon these rocks to die.

On a Guano Island.

All this has been going on for many years, and the result is a deposit which is so valuable as manure that ships are sent here to take it away to our country and to Europe. There are houses upon some of the islands, put up for the men who dig out the guano, and on one or two of them there are little railroads which have been made to carry the guano down to the shores.

XIV. ALONG THE COAST TO VALPARAISO.

IT takes us five days by steamer to go from Iquique to Valparaiso (väl-pä-rī'sō), the chief seaport of Chile. The sail along the west coast is delightful. There are few storms, and almost every day we make a new port, at which we see many strange things.

Luscious grapes and oranges are brought to the steamer from the valley oases of the desert, and we now and then take on a few barrels of wine.

While our steamer stops at Antofagasta we have time to visit the largest smelter in all South America. It has been built here to smelt the silver out of the ore brought down from the Andes. This work is done in huge furnaces, the ore being melted with other materials in such a way that the pure silver is taken out of the rocks.

The ore is first ground to powder, which is then molded into bricks. As we pass through the yard we see a large plot of ground upon which are piled up enough bricks to build a big house. It is perhaps the richest brickyard on earth. The bricks look like blocks of gray sand, but they are really silver ore, ground fine and molded into this shape that the ore may be more easily smelted.

Farther down the coast we anchor at Coquimbo (kō-kēm'bō) to take on a big load of copper. Hundreds of long bars or bricks of reddish-brown metal are brought out to our steamer on a lighter and put away in the hold.

This copper comes from mines not far from the town. We learn that Chile has vast deposits of very rich copper. It lies in great lumps or veins in the mountains, and is dug out and smelted in the furnaces at this port and elsewhere.

Soon after leaving Coquimbo we notice that the shores have lost their gray, dusty look. Now and then we see a tree and a patch of green grass. We are out of the desert at last.

We sail about two hundred miles farther south, and finally come to anchor in the Bay of Valparaiso. It is shaped like a half-moon, being walled with steep hills covered with luxuriant trees and beautiful flowers. A few miles inland from the coast there are orange and lemon groves, vineyards and trees bearing almost all kinds of fruits; and just over the mountains is the long valley of Chile, one of the richest farming and fruit-raising regions of all South America.

At Valparaiso we are not halfway along the coast. Chile extends from here to the Strait of Magellan. It is the narrowest of all countries in proportion to its length. It stretches only from the ocean to the top of the Andes, and its width is nowhere greater than the distance from New York to Boston. In some places, indeed, its width is not greater than the distance from Philadelphia to New York, but it is so long that if laid from east to west upon the United States, with one end at New York, it would stretch out far beyond Great Salt Lake. If you could twist it around, so that it would lie north and south, with Tierra del Fuego on the Florida Keys, the nitrate fields which we have just left would be in Hudson Bay, about even with the northern part of Labrador.

A land of this kind must have many climates. It was quite hot at Iquique, but the winter air here at Valparaiso is pleasantly cool, and near the Strait of Magellan the ground is often covered with snow. The same difference

Harbor, Valparaiso.

exists in regard to rain. In the northern desert one never needs an umbrella, but at Valparaiso it rains now and then throughout the year. It rains more as you go farther south, and in some places so much water falls that the people jokingly say it rains thirteen months every year.

As we reach the rain belt the desert suddenly stops; green fields are frequently seen; and as we go still farther south we shall travel in a valley covered with crops, and come into a country where the grass grows luxuriantly and where there are great forests bound together with vines.

But what is the cause of the change? Why is northern Chile so dry and the greater part of southern Chile wet?

It comes from the winds. We have learned that the

desert exists because the winds which come from the east have had the water squeezed out of them by the cold air of the mountains before they reach the west slope.

The winds which roll over southern Chile come from a different direction. They are blown toward the southeast. As they cross the warm waters of the Pacific they drink themselves full of moisture, and when they reach the cold part of Chile the difference in the temperature makes this moisture drop down. Hence we shall find that there are copious rains, producing many streams, which flow down the west slope of the Andes. On the other side of the mountains, in parts of Patagonia, the country is almost a desert, for the winds have been wrung dry before they reach there.

Leaving our ship, we explore Valparaiso. The city is about the size of Indianapolis. It is the best business point upon the whole coast, owing its growth to its harbor, which is large enough to float all the ships of the world.

We come to anchor among steamers from different parts of Europe. They are loading and discharging goods. Some of them are taking on cattle, wheat, vegetables, and fruits for the cities of the desert farther north, and others have stopped on their way to add to their cargoes of nitrate, copper, and hides, which they will carry from Chile to Europe.

We take a boat to the shore, wondering how we can get up the hills to the houses above us. Valparaiso rises from the water in the shape of an amphitheater, or like the grand stand of a ball ground. The streets rise in terraces, one above the other, so that the buildings at the top seem to hang out above and threaten to fall down upon those below.

But see, there are cable cars climbing up and down the

steep hills. It is by them we shall mount from one street to another, for the only level land in the city is a narrow stretch along the shore.

Upon this level place is the business part of Valparaiso. It is all on made ground. The hills were dug down and the waters kept back by walls of stone and iron rails, in order that the tide might not eat out the land.

Chileans.

We step from our boat upon stone wharves, and walk over streets as well paved as our streets at home. It is hard for us to believe we are in a South American city. The buildings are large and much like those of our cities. The stores have plate glass windows. We see German and English names over some of them, and we learn that Valparaiso has many Europeans who have come here to engage in trade.

The people do not look much different from those of New York and Chicago. There are electric lights. We hear the boys cry the newspapers, and as we notice the signs of enterprise all about us we believe what has been told us, that the Chileans are among the most enterprising people of the South American continent.

The country contains about three million inhabitants.

They do not call themselves Chileans, but Chilenos (chelā'nos), and they pride themselves on being better and stronger than the people of the countries farther north.

They are like them, however, in that they are the descendants of the Spaniards and of the mixed race of Spaniards and Indians. The difference is that the Spaniards who came to Chile were chiefly from the northern provinces of Spain, where the people are stronger and better than those of the south, and also that the Chilean Indians were the famed Araucanians, a much stronger and braver race than the tribes ruled by the Incas, with whom the Spaniards united in Ecuador and Peru.

Street Scene, Valparaiso

The Chileans we see on the streets of Valparaiso are dressed just as we are. We hear many of them speak

English, and as we look at our familiar surroundings we wonder whether Chile is, after all, much different from the United States.

But stop. There comes a lady with a black shawl draped about her head, and behind her is a vegetable peddler with his stock in panniers on the sides of a mule. There is a bread mule being dragged along by the baker, and a milk mule going down that side street. Get out of the way of that carriage with its high-stepping horses, and, as you do so, look out for the horse which has just come around the corner. Its rider is a man with a poncho and a broad-brimmed hat. He is probably a rich farmer in from the country. We shall see many of his kind later on.

"A queer street car."

What a queer street car that is going by us! It has seats on top as well as inside. See that pretty woman on the rear platform. She is the conductor. She is taking up the fares and making change from the money in her white apron pocket. There are women street car conductors in all of the chief cities of Chile. The custom was introduced when Chile was at war with Peru and the men were all needed for soldiers.

But we may as well leave Valparaiso. It has so many foreigners that we must go inland to see how the Chileans live and to learn about their country. There are railroads to the interior, and we decide to make our first journey on the Transandine line.

XV. ACROSS SOUTH AMERICA BY RAIL.

WE have already seen something of the railroads farther north which go from the Pacific to the top of the Andes. The one upon which we are riding to-day will soon join the Atlantic and Pacific oceans together. It is the Transandine Railroad, going over the Andes from Valparaiso to Buenos Aires.

Our car is a Pullman, and we can see well as we go. Leaving Valparaiso, the train skirts the edge of the harbor, passing through the rich suburb of Vina del Mar.

How soft the air is, and how sweet the smell of the trees and grass after our long stay in the desert! Morning-glories are blooming on the fences at the roadside, and that great bush over there is loaded with roses. Now we whiz by an orange grove, almost close enough to grab at the yellow balls peeping out of the leaves. Now we go by vineyards, and now we stop at a station, at which pears,

Transandine Railroad.

figs, and lemons are brought to the car windows for sale. How cheap everything is! We can get a big bunch of grapes, or all the oranges we can eat, for a dime.

Now the road leaves the coast, and we are climbing the hills. There is but little green except in the valleys. They are covered with cultivated fields, through which flow irrigating ditches supplied by the streams.

See the men at work in the fields. There is one plowing. He has two white oxen joined to the plow by a pole. The pole is tied to the yoke, which rests on the necks of the oxen just back of the horns, to which it is fastened with skin ropes.

At the next station we see oxen yoked the same way pulling huge carts loaded with grain. Notice the wheels of the carts. They are twice as high as those of our carts, and the loads are so heavy that eight oxen are yoked in double file to each cart. How the wheels creak and screech on their way past the train! The oxen are pushing their burden along by their heads. The method of yoking them is cruel indeed. An ox cannot move his head unless his fellow ox moves at the same time.

A Load of Grain.

The houses of the Chilean towns are very similar to those we saw on the coast of Peru. There are many huts in the fields, made of mud, with roofs of straw, thatch, or sheet iron.

After we cross the coast range the farms are larger and the country is more thickly populated. We ride for some time through the irrigated valley of the Aconcagua river, with the mighty mountains rising above us. We are now climbing the second range of the Andes.

As we go on, gradually rising, we pass orchards of apples and peaches, with rich, well-watered gardens lying high up in the mountains. The country grows wilder and wilder, and at last we are at the station where the road ends.

We are now very near the frontier of Argentina and within a short distance of the long Argentina Railroad, which crosses the pampas to Buenos Aires. We have not

Uspallata Pass.

time now to make the whole journey, for we wish to go about through the southern part of the continent by the Strait of Magellan. So we shall merely ride over the mountains on mules, to look at the other end of the road, and then return to our travels in Chile. The railroad is not yet completed, but the distance between the two sections is so short that we can go there and back in less than three days.

Wagon Road up the Andes.

This road over the Andes is by the Uspallata Pass, which is 12,340 feet above the sea. It is a fairly good mountain road in the summer, but now, in the winter, it is often blocked up with deep snows. At times the snows are so heavy that all travel is stopped. The mails pile up at the two ends of the railroad, and the mail carriers going between them are sometimes lost in the storm.

CARP. S. AM.—8

That is why the little stone huts which we pass now and then have been built. They have no windows. They look more like bake ovens than houses. They are for shelter for the passengers and postmen who are caught in the storms. Men sometimes have to live in them for days, waiting for the snows to melt in the mountains.

There are one or two rude inns on the way, where we stop; the hot soup tastes good, for we are cold.

The Andes at this point are wild in the extreme. One of the worst parts of the pass is called the Valley of Desolation. Here the land is covered with volcanic rock, upon which nothing can grow. Now and then we see a guanaco, a wild animal which looks somewhat like a llama, except that its fur is yellow spotted with white. We shall see more such farther south.

Now a condor soars about over us. There it is between us and the sun, casting a shadow upon the snow. Condors when they are hungry are like vultures; they will eat dead things, and we are wondering whether that mighty bird is not waiting to see us drop in our tracks.

A Condor.

How pure the air is, and how thin! We fear we may have another attack of mountain sickness. We are, however, more than a mile lower down at the summit of this pass than at the Galera tunnel, through which we crossed the Andes on the Oroya Railroad back of Lima, and our faintness soon passes off.

The highest part of the Transandine Railroad, yet to be built, will include many tunnels. The cars will be taken up the steepest part of the mountain by a track like those which go up Pikes Peak and Mount Washington. The track will have three rails. In addition to the two which you usually see on a railroad there will be a third narrow rail with many rungs in it, like a ladder. Upon this a cog wheel attached to the car will move, and the little engine made for the purpose will be behind the train instead of in front of it. The cars will be pushed, not pulled, up the mountains. At about two miles above the sea there will be a tunnel through the mountains, and there will also be many snowsheds cut out of the solid rock, through which the trains will pass in order that they may not be stopped in the winter.

The road will be of great good to South American travelers. We shall see this as we go by the old route around the south end of the continent to Buenos Aires. The voyage from Valparaiso by the Strait of Magellan takes from fourteen to sixteen days. When this road is finished passengers will be carried clear across the continent in twenty-nine hours. It will make the trip from Europe to the west coast of South America very much shorter, and travelers from Europe to Australia will come to Buenos Aires in about twenty days, then cross South America by rail, and take ship at Valparaiso, instead of making the long voyage around through the Strait of Magellan as they now do.

On our journey over the road we have fine views of

Aconcagua, the highest of the Andes. It is one of the fine mountain sights of the world. When the sky is clear it can be seen from Valparaiso rising in a great cone high above the others of the Chilean Andes, dwarfing all the

Aconcagua.

peaks near it except Mount Tupungato (too - poon - gä′tō), which is more than four miles in height.

Aconcagua is more than 23,900 feet high, and as we look at its snowy top we long to climb it. If we should make the attempt, we should probably meet snowstorms, and we might be frozen during the cold nights.

Near the summit there are cliffs which are hard to scale, and at the top we should stand on a square plateau about two hundred feet wide, with great masses of fleecy clouds far below us, and the mountains stretching away to the east and to the south. On one side we could see the pampas of Argentina, and on the other, over the narrow band of green which is the country of Chile, ninety miles away, would be the shining, silvery waters of the Pacific.

This journey, however, can be made only in the summer, and our guides will not allow us to make the attempt. We must be satisfied with the magnificent views we have had as we rode through the pass. So we remount our mules and slowly climb back down the hills to the railroad. Here we take the train for Los Andes, where we change cars to the line which goes down the central valley of Chile and brings us at last to Santiago.

XVI. SANTIAGO, THE CAPITAL OF CHILE.

SANTIAGO (sän-tĭ-ä′gō) is the capital of Chile. It is almost as large as our national capital, and in many things like it. Washington is six hours distant from our chief seaport, New York. Santiago is about six hours by rail from Valparaiso, the chief seaport of Chile. Washington lies in a basin on the banks of the Potomac. Santiago is cut in two by the river Mapo′cho, and the basin upon which it is built is walled by the snowy Andes and by low mountains which rise one above another from grassy plains.

We have our Capitol Hill. Santiago has its Santa Lucia (loo-sē′ä), a mass of volcanic rocks rising almost precipitously in the midst of the city to a height more than half that of the Washington Monument.

Santa Lucia is perhaps the most picturesque hill of any city of the world. It has a base of a little more than an acre. It is composed of rocks enormous in size and piled together in curious shapes. There is earth mixed with the rocks, so that trees grow among them. Flowers and vines have been planted, and the hill has been made into a beautiful park. Its sides are covered with English ivy. Tall eucalyptus trees rise out of the crevices of the rocks from its base to its summit. It has wonderful ferns, dark caves, and beautiful grottoes in which there are waterfalls, making altogether what might be called a hanging garden away up there above the city, under the shadow of the Andes.

There are winding driveways and footpaths which go round and round the hill to the summit. We walk up one

Santa Lucia.

of the paths to take a look over Santiago. It is early morning, and the sun is just rising up in the great blue dome of the sky. It has caught the tops of the Andes at the back of the city, and the snows upon them are shining like frosted silver incrusted with diamonds. The foothills in the shadow are like blue velvet, and we look at the plains away off in the distance, with their rich growth of green.

Our eyes now drop to the city below us. Red-tiled roofs with trees and bushes growing out of them extend about on all sides. Those are the roofs of the Chilean capital. The scene is not unlike that we saw from the top of our hotel in Lima. The houses are built in the same style. They are close to the streets, and consist of rooms built around small courts, or patios, in which are the gardens. Some of the Santiago houses are of vast size, although all are low, few being of more than two stories.

"The Alameda, the chief street of this South American capital."

See that wide avenue which cuts the city almost in halves. That is the Alameda, the chief street of this South American capital. It is twice as wide as Pennsylvania Avenue in Washington. There are rows of tall poplar trees running through it from one end to the other, and along each side of the trees are stone aqueducts in which streams of mountain water are flowing.

With our field glasses we see the statues of many Chilean heroes under the trees, and at every few feet stone seats upon which men and women are sitting, enjoying the air. Boys are riding on bicycles along the paths in the center of the street, and at every few hundred feet there are two or three cows with their calves beside them. Each of the calves wears a muzzle. The cows are owned by women, who milk them from time to time and sell the milk warm from the cow to the people who are out taking the air. The cows are not tied, but are hobbled by ropes about their hind legs.

Now turn your eyes a little more to the right. There is another wide strip of green, with a band of silver running through it. That is the river Mapocho, which flows through the city. A little more to the left is the race course, which is thronged by thousands on Sunday afternoons, when the chief races are held. The forest above it is Cousiño (coo-zēn'yo) Park, where the people drive in their carriages every afternoon.

But let us go down from the hill and take a street car ride through the city. The seats on the roof of the car are the best for sight-seeing, and to ride there costs only one cent of our money per trip.

Think of a street car ride for a cent, and that ride through Santiago! We give our fare to the woman conductor, and are soon whizzing along, as high up as the roofs of the one-story houses, through the suburbs and poorer parts of the town. Now we pass between the higher buildings of the business section. What fine stores they are! They are as good as our stores at home. The show windows have all sorts of beautiful goods, and there are several great arcades roofed with glass which have been cut through the business blocks from one side to the other.

"Let us take a street car ride through the city."

We go by the Moneda, or the mint. It is a great building which contains also the home of the president and most of the offices of the Chilean government. At the door there are soldiers with drawn swords in their hands. Later on we see that the president of Chile has a military guard of two hundred cavalry which goes with his carriage on all state occasions.

The Chileans are fond of pomp and display. We meet policemen with swords at their sides on every street corner, and we shall see soldiers drilling in every city and town.

Chile is a republic after the South American fashion, in

which the chief families control the elections and hold most of the offices.

In that building we are now passing the houses of Congress meet, and those men who are going in are senators and deputies who sit there and make laws just as in our Congress at home.

But here we are at the Plaza des Armes, where all the cars stop. This is the center of the Chilean capital. That big building over there is the cathedral, and the great

"In that building the houses of Congress meet."

structure next door is the palace where the archbishop lives. The Roman Catholic religion is the chief religion of Chile, and the church has a great deal of property. Some of the best business blocks of Santiago belong to it, and it has vast estates in the country, upon which fruit and wheat and other such things are raised for sale. Those ladies dressed all in black, with black shawls on their heads, are going to mass. See the little rugs which they have with them. They kneel upon them when they pray, for many of the churches have no seats, and the stone floors are cold.

Later on we visit the schools. They are much like our schools at home, save that the girls and the boys are kept in different buildings, and that the children of the lower grades all study out loud. Chile has now a good public school system. There are schools in every city and village, although four children out of every five are still kept at home. We find Santiago has a national university with a thousand students, and that there are also schools for the army and navy.

Indeed, we are surprised at the intelligence of the Chileans. They have been called the Yankees of South America, because they are so bright and enterprising and in other ways like us. Many people of the better classes speak French and English, some having been educated in Europe. In all the cities there are daily newspapers. We meet newsboys on almost every street corner, and visit large bookstores in the business parts of the city.

At the post office we learn that millions of letters and newspapers go through the mails every year, and when we inquire we find that there are telegraph lines to all parts of the country, and that the prices for telegrams are much lower than we pay at home. There are electric lights and electric railroads in the principal Chilean cities. Telephones are to be found in all the large towns, and you can talk from Santiago to your friends in Valparaiso over the telephone, although it is distant six hours by rail.

During our stay at the capital we are invited to visit the homes of some well-to-do Chileans. We are surprised at the size of their houses. They are of one or two stories, but many of them have forty large rooms, which are furnished as expensively as the houses of our millionaires. In many homes we see fine paintings and statues, and in the suburbs we visit mansions with gardens about them, in which are lemon and orange trees and all kinds of beautiful flowers.

But how about the poor? All of the Chileans cannot be rich. No, indeed; they are not. There are poor people everywhere. We see them driving carts, and carrying goods on their backs through the streets. We shall find them living in mud huts in all parts of the country, and if we will again mount to the top of the street car we may ride through sections of Santiago which are filled with low one-story houses in which whole families live in one room.

Many of the poor people sleep on the floor, and their food costs but a few cents a day. They are mostly of the mixed race of Spanish and Indians. They do the hard work of Chile, and we shall see much of them in our trips through the country.

XVII. A VISIT TO A CHILEAN FARM.

TO-DAY we start down the great central valley of Chile. This valley lies between the main range of the Andes and the mountains which border the coast. It is in places over a hundred miles wide, and as long as the distance from New York to Pittsburg. It is divided into vast estates, upon which all sorts of fruits and grains are grown, and where cattle and horses are grazed in droves of thousands.

There are few countries in the world where farms are so large as in Chile, or their owners so rich. We meet men who each own thousands of acres, and see many estates which are worth more than a million dollars. The wealthier farmers live like lords upon their estates or haciendas. Farming is profitable in Chile. The country produces every year more than twenty-eight million bushels of wheat, millions of gallons of wine, and the best horses and cattle on the west coast of South America.

More than half of the people of Chile are engaged in farming, but only a few families own land. Most of the farms are in this great central valley. They are irri-

Hay Wagon.

gated by the streams from the mountains, and are in most places cultivated like gardens. The fields are divided by canals, along which trees have been planted. Some of the estates have stone walls about them, and now and then we see a fence of wire or boards. We look in vain for barns and haystacks and farmhouses like our own. The only buildings are the vast one-story structures of the owners and the mud huts of the workmen. Oxen everywhere take the place of horses and mules. Huge carts drawn by oxen with yokes tied to their horns are used instead of farm wagons, and the plows are dragged through the furrows by the same clumsy beasts.

Some of the more enterprising Chileans, however, have been introducing modern machinery lately, and some of the rich farmers now have American plows, threshers, and reapers.

We visit one of the farms, where we are the guests of the proprietor. He has given us rooms in his country home, which he occupies only in the summer time, when he lives on his country estate.

Chilean Farmer.

What a lot of rooms there are! There must be a hundred all told, and all on the ground floor. The buildings are of one story, with roofs of red tiles, mud walls, and brick floors. They surround little green courts and gardens. Groves of trees, some of which are one hundred feet high, are growing about them.

There are many other guests at the time of our visit. There are about thirty children among them, and when

"There are horses for all."

we go out to ride there are horses for all, some of the little ones being tied to the saddles of their ponies to keep them from falling, for the children here learn to ride when quite young.

Every child of a rich farmer has its own pony, and we see boys and girls between the ages of four and fourteen galloping over the fields, holding their seats like men and women.

The farm is so large that we might ride all day on the roads which go through the fields and not visit the whole. The fields are divided by fences of stone and also by canals, along which have been planted Lombardy poplars, which so shade the road that we do not feel the warm sun.

We are delighted with the horses. The peons chase them on the gallop over the fields to show us how well they can run. They are fine riding animals. They are trained to a gait much like a pace, but so easy that we remain in our saddles for hours without fatigue. The horses are directed by pressing the reins against the sides of the neck, and not by pulling at the bit, and the lines are usually left loose. As a result the horses are seldom hard in the mouth.

The saddles are much heavier than ours. Many of them are plated with silver, and ladies and gentlemen frequently use silver stirrups. A Chilean often cares more to have his horse well dressed than to be well dressed himself. His bridle bit is of silver, and his spurs are often of the same metal. The spurs used by the peons have rowels, or spiked wheels, as big around as a coffee cup. Some have wheels four inches in diameter, so that they cause great pain if the owner is cruel.

Later on we go to the cattle. There are great herds of fine stock and flocks of fat sheep. The crops in the fields are growing luxuriantly, and the vineyards and orange orchards are loaded with fruits.

We ask how such a place is managed, and are told that it has a major-domo, or chief, who has overseers under him and who organizes his laborers much like an army. Each overseer has so many men to take charge of, and he tells each man what to do. Books are kept showing just how much money is paid out and what is

"There are great herds of fine stock."

done every day, so that the proprietor knows how well each field is paying.

Indeed, the only poor things on the farm are the rotos, or farm workmen. The rotos are the laboring class of the country. They are somewhat like the Indians we saw in Peru and Bolivia. They come of the mixed race of Spaniards and Indians, inheriting the bravery of both. Peruvian and Bolivian Indians are afraid of their masters; the Chilean rotos are not. They carry knives, and the master who should strike one of them would probably be stabbed in return. It is said, however, that the rotos love their masters. They do not often leave the estates upon which they were born.

Let us enter one of their huts. What a contrast to the luxurious city home of the owner! The walls are of mud bricks, and the roof is of thatch. The ground forms the floor, and in this case the bed of the family. Two boxes and a table are the only furniture. The hut has but one room, about fifteen feet square, and we are told that a family of eight lives in it.

We wonder how people can exist in such quarters, and when we learn what they eat we wonder more. Their first meal usually consists of a double handful of toasted wheat flour mixed with water into a mush or baked as a cake. At noon they have a bowl of hot beans, and for

"We wonder how people can exist in such quarters."

supper, or dinner, as they call it, a second bowl of beans, to which is added some toasted meal. They seldom eat meat, preferring to spend their money for drink.

As a result of this mode of living many of the roto children die. Only the strongest survive, but those who grow up are so strong that four rotos can easily lift a piano on their heads and trot away with it.

The rotos are very polite. When not drunk they are kind to their families. They are always ready to help one another in trouble. It is difficult to teach them habits of thrift, but it is hoped that through the common schools, which have recently been introduced into all parts of Chile, they will become educated and in time be a much better race.

XVIII. SOUTHERN CHILE AND THE ARAUCANIANS.

WE have left our friends in the country and are again on the train. We travel several hundred miles southward through the great central valley. The snowy Andes are still on our left, with smoke rising here and there from a volcanic peak. We cross little rivers and travel through vast wheat fields cut up by ditches in which the clear water flows.

What a lot of vineyards there are! The hills are covered with low grapevines, now brown and leafless, for it is winter. See that drove of cattle at the side of the road, with the rotos on horseback driving the animals this way and that. They are rounding up, or counting, the stock and branding the young with red-hot irons. There are a thousand horses in the next field, and we shall pass other cattle and horses between the stations on our way farther south.

What queer trees border the fields! They are lofty poplars planted along the irrigating ditches, all leaning north, blown so by the winds, which usually come from the south. They look like hedges, and form lines of green a hundred feet high running between the great fields.

What is this broad stream we are crossing? It is the Biobio (bē-o-bē′o), the largest river of Chile. It rises in the Andes, not far from the Argentina boundary, and

Bridge over the Biobio.

flows across the country, emptying into the Bay of Concepcion. How wide it is! The steel bridge over which we cross is one of the finest in South America; it seems to us more than a mile long.

There are woods on the banks of the Biobio, and from now on we shall frequently be in the forests. There are no more irrigating ditches, for the rains furnish plenty of water.

See the big trees on both sides of the railroad. We have at last come into the forest region of Chile, which extends from here to the Strait of Magellan.

The wheat fields we are now passing have been cut out of the woods. How large they are! They look like our fields in the new lands of the Northwest. There are stumps in them. The houses of the poor are log cabins. We see men at work cutting down the trees. Those long teams of oxen are dragging out lumber, their big, soft eyes looking sadly at us as they painfully pull the heavy loads along by their heads.

Notice the people at the station. How different they seem from the rotos we saw in the north! They are dark-faced and fierce-looking. They are more warmly clad. The men wear ponchos, and many have on high boots covered with mud.

Listen to that group at the corner. The men are talking German, and they do not look like Chileans. They are German settlers who have come here from Europe to farm the land, which the Chilean government sells to immigrants at a very low price. We shall see more Germans in the towns of this part of Chile. At Valdivia there are large tanneries, in which German workmen make fine leather for shipment to Hamburg and Russia. The trees about us have good bark for tanning, and Chile has so many cattle that hides are cheap.

But who are the copper-colored people we meet everywhere? They wear gorgeous ponchos woven in stripes of bright colors. The women have bare arms. Their dresses seem to be long blankets wrapped tightly over their chests and falling down to their feet. Some have square earrings of silver, half as big as a schoolbook and as thick as one of its covers. Others have silver plates on their bosoms, and bands of silver beads about their necks and their ankles. They look like Indians, but they are not dressed like our Indians at home.

They are Indians. They are the descendants of the famed Araucanians, who inhabited Chile at the time the Spaniards first came. They were noted for their bravery, and it is said that more Spanish lives were lost in attempts

"They are the descendants of the famed Araucanians."

to conquer them than in all the wars for the conquests of Mexico and Peru. Their struggle with the Spaniards lasted more than a century, and ended by leaving to the Araucanians a great part of southern Chile.

Since then some of this has been taken away year after year, and now the lands of the Araucanians are few.

Alcohol furnished by the whites has made them a nation of drunkards, and their bad habits are fast killing them off. They are now less in number than when they first fought the Spaniards, and they grow fewer and fewer each year.

The Araucanians have different tribes, commanded by chiefs, although many of them live on farms of their own. We leave our train and visit one of their homes. The

"We visit one of their homes."

house is more like a shed than anything else. It contains but one room about twenty feet square, and it has no wall at all at the front, the open side being faced away from the wind. Skins are drawn over this side when the weather is cold.

Take a look at the roof. It is made of skins and straw thatch. The walls are of logs, and the floor is of dirt.

Let us go in. How black everything is! You can hardly see about you for the dense smoke which comes from that fire in the middle of the hut. It is built in a hole in the ground, and the smoke finds its way out as it can.

The squaw who bends over the fire is cooking the dinner. She has a pot on the coals, in which she is stewing mutton and vegetables cut up in small pieces.

Now the meal is ready, and our host asks us to sit down and eat with him. We squat on the floor, and each takes a spoon and dips the stew out of the pot. The women of the family do not dine with us. The men always eat first, the Indian women standing behind them like servants and taking what is left. How hot the stew is! It is full of red pepper, and it brings the tears to our eyes.

But who is that woman who has come in during the meal and started another fire farther back in the hut? That is our host's other wife. An Araucanian often has more than one wife, and in such cases each wife cooks for herself. There are two beds on the different sides of the room, curtained off with fur rugs or blankets. Each bed belongs to a wife, in which she sleeps with her own children about her.

The Araucanians have queer notions of courtship. Marriage with them is largely a matter of bargain and sale. A father expects a lot of presents of cattle, sheep, or horses for his daughter, and until these are promised he will not consent to the marriage.

After all is settled the young man comes some dark night to the house of his sweetheart and carries her off. The girl usually knows he is coming, and though she may want to be married, she pretends she does not. She has her friends with her, and when her lover and his friends break in, there is a fight between the men and the women. The men try to carry off the girl, and the girl and her friends use all their powers of resistance. At last the groom drags the bride out. He swings her upon his horse, and jumping behind her, goes off on the gallop, making for the nearest woods. The girl's friends follow shrieking behind, but the groom of course soon distances them. Having reached the forest, he takes his lady love into its recesses, and there they spend a few days. After this short honeymoon they return to the house of the groom, and are then looked upon as married. The husband now takes his presents to the father of his wife, and the young couple settle down.

The women we meet seem to be happy. They are kind to their children and are fond of them. The children laugh and play just as our children do, and we laugh ourselves when we see the little papooses smiling at us out of the bundles in which they are tied.

"The mother carries it on her back."

Almost as soon as one of these Indian babies is born it is wrapped in a skin or cloth and tied to a framework about a yard high and so wide that it will easily rest on the back of its mother. The mother carries it on her back by a strap which runs around her head, and when she is tired she takes off the strap and stands the papoose against a tree or the wall of her hut. She keeps it thus tied up until it is able to walk, carrying it with her wherever she goes.

Some of the Indian women are skilled in weaving. They spin their own wool and weave their own clothes,

They make beautiful blankets, weaving them in stripes of red, black, and blue.

We spend a day moving about over their farms, and notice that the men at work in the fields are often of the mixed race. The Indians employ them to work for them rather than labor themselves.

XIX. IN THE COAL MINES OF CHILE.

WE have left the land of the Araucanians and are now in the city of Concepcion. It is the chief port of southern Chile. It lies a few miles back from Arauco Bay, where we expect to get a ship for the Strait of Magellan.

Concepcion is the greatest commercial city of southern Chile, and its people say it will soon be the chief seaport of the southern Pacific. It has two excellent harbors, Arauco Bay and Talcahuano (täl-kä-wah′no), which are near by, and it is so connected by railroads with all parts of the country that it has a great trade. The city has about fifty thousand people. It is a flat Spanish town with a plaza in the center, and streets which cross one another at right angles.

This part of Chile is especially important because it contains some of the chief coal fields of the Pacific coast of South America. There is but little coal on the coast, and coal is brought here by the shipload from Australia and England. The coal fields of Chile lie along the ocean shore for a distance of almost one hundred miles. The coal is not so good as that which is brought from abroad, and it must be sold at a lower price. The mines are so close to the sea, however, that they can be worked at a profit.

COAL MINES.

Street Scene, Concepcion.

It is for coal that the steamer for the Strait of Magellan has stopped in Arauco Bay. She now lies at anchor near Lota, with great barges of coal by her side. We see sooty-faced rotos standing in the barges and shoveling the coal on board.

The ship is bound for Hamburg. She must force her way through the ocean, a distance of about five thousand miles, before she can get coal again. It takes a vast deal of fuel to make steam for such a big ship. This vessel uses more in one day than many families can consume in a year, and it will keep the rotos shoveling until night to load up.

As we go on board the captain tells us we have time to visit one of the mines. We are tired, and at first think it hardly worth while, until the captain says that the coal beds of this region slope from the land down under the ocean, and that the coal which they are now shoveling on board comes from under the sea.

This seems very strange. So we call a small boat which is near the ship, waiting for passengers, to take us on shore.

We are soon landed at the entrance to one of the greatest of the coal mines. The works above ground consist of

Entrance to a Coal Mine.

large buildings situated upon little islands connected with the coast by a railroad built upon piers. We tell the manager that we wish to visit his mine, and he kindly sends a guide with us.

We are taken to a great shaft or well in which, by a steam engine and pulleys, two elevators are raising cars filled with coal and lowering empty cars to the bottom.

We step upon the elevator that is just going down, and drop into darkness. Down, down, down we go, until at last rays of light shoot up from below us. Our speed grows slower, and we stop before a long tunnel with a line of electric lights extending on and on in front of us, growing less and less in size until they fade into stars in the distance.

As we step out of the shaft a train of loaded cars comes thundering toward us, and we see that they are moved by an overhead trolley like the electric street cars of some of our cities.

But there is another train going back. Can we get on? Yes; a special car with seats upon it has been attached to the train for us. We climb upon the platform, and speed away over the track at the rate of twenty miles an hour. Within a few moments we leave the shore, and are soon far out under the bed of the Pacific Ocean.

We are moving along through a tunnel which has been cut out of the great sheet of coal which lies down here between the layers of rock. As we go on we pass openings to the right and to the left. They are the entrances to tunnels, which have been made to cut out the coal.

Think where we are! We are hundreds of feet down under the ocean, and big steamers are floating above us. And still it is dry. There is not a drop on our clothes or our hats, for the great beds of rock just over the cars are such that the water cannot get through.

As we ride on, now and then a train passes. In the tunnels at the sides we see half-naked miners covered with dirt, digging out the coal and loading it upon cars.

What is that boom, boom, boom which sounds as though the sea were breaking in through the rocks away at the right? That is from the blasting done to get out the coal. There is no danger where we are now, but we must look out, for if such an explosion occurred near us it might blow us to pieces.

What a great mine this is! There are hundreds of men

at work in it, and vast quantities of coal are taken out every day.

We return to the shaft on a train with twenty-seven cars of coal in front of us, and another train arrives while we are waiting to ride to the top.

Again we are back on the steamer. It is almost ready to sail. It has loaded nine hundred tons of coal in the last twenty-four hours. Its freight has been packed away

"In the tunnels we see half-naked miners."

during its calls at the various ports farther north, and within a few moments it will start on its long voyage to Europe around through the Strait of Magellan.

It is a big ship, and it carries a vast deal of freight. Below deck are three thousand tons of nitrate of soda, two thousand barrels of liquid honey, and great rolls of sole leather, all going to Europe. We have wheat, wine, and flour for Punta Arenas, on the Strait of Magellan, and similar freight for Buenos Aires and Montevideo.

Everything is carefully packed, for we are now going into some of the stormiest seas of the world. The extreme southern end of the continent may be called the very home of the winds. About Cape Horn fierce winds blow all the year through. There are many storms farther north, and seamen are glad when they reach the Strait of Magellan, in which the waters are usually quiet. It is by the Strait of Magellan that we shall go, and our steamer will avoid some of the storms by traveling through the narrow channels which run in and out among the mountainous islands along the west coast. This is the Smythes Channel route, the scenery of which is wonderfully grand.

We are anxious to be off, and are glad when, as evening falls, there is a rattling of chains and the anchor is raised. We hear the thump, thump, thump of the engines, and as we go to bed we are moving out of the smooth waters of Arauco Bay into the ocean.

We awake to find the ship rolling. We have to hold to our berths while we dress, and a lurch of the vessel often sends us against the walls of our rooms.

We climb upstairs to the deck, and bracing ourselves against the rail look out over the sea. There are whitecaps everywhere. The waves rise and fall in huge masses. They whip the ship, striking its sides with a noise like a cannon. Now a great wave dashes over the lower deck, and now a still higher one splashes over the top, flooding everything and making us run to our cabins.

When we sit down at dinner there is a network of slats upon the table to hold the plates, cups, and other dishes, that a lurch of the ship may not send them into our laps. We lift our soup plates halfway to our mouths and balance them with the roll of the vessel, trying at the same time to get our spoons between our lips without spilling the soup.

How few of the girls have come down to dinner! They are more subject to seasickness than the boys, and prefer to stay in bed in their cabins. Some of the boys are seasick too, and even the bravest of us does not care quite so much for his food as he did upon land.

A day or so later we have grown used to the motion and are all upon deck. We enjoy the changes which the rough sea and the storms bring every hour. Now we are shrouded in mist, and every few minutes the foghorn blows to warn other ships to keep out of our way. Now the fog lifts, and we see high waves rolling about on all sides. There is a break in the clouds, and away off to the east is a faint line of blue. That is the long, narrow island of Chiloë (chē-lō-ā'); the mainland is much farther off. We are fortunate in securing a view, for in the winter in Chiloë the natives say it rains six days every week, and on the seventh the sky is much overcast. In the summer there are a few pleasant days, but even then the island is half shrouded in mist.

There is more fog and snow as we sail on southward. The sea is still rough, and we cannot safely walk about the deck until we enter the Gulf of Peñas, from which we are to sail inward on our way through Smythes Channel.

It is only four o'clock when we enter the gulf, but it is already quite dark. We are now so far south that in winter night begins very early, and the electric lights are already turned on. The ship moves very gently, and when we go to sleep we feel no more motion than when in our own beds at home.

XX. IN AND ABOUT THE STRAIT OF MAGELLAN.

WE have been moving slowly all night, and awake to find the waves gone. We have left the open Pacific and are passing through the series of channels, about four hundred miles long, which winds in and out among the islands of western Patagonia and will bring us at last to the Strait of Magellan.

The scenes about us are among the grandest of the world. There are mountains on all sides. We are sailing amongst their tops and are in a land of clouds. The channel is more like a narrow river than a branch of the ocean. It carries us in and out among rocky, grass-clad islands. On our left, ragged mountains of curious shapes rise almost straight up from the water. Their sides near the shore are green, and we see they are matted with moss and evergreen trees. Higher up, the green is dusted with snow, and at the top there is ice. Some of the peaks are half hidden in vapor. Others, nearer our vessel, stand out bold and clear—great masses of dark-green velvet under a lavender sky.

As we sail on the scenery changes. The mountains assume curious shapes, and we imagine pictures in them such as you sometimes see in the clouds. There is one that looks like the Great Pyramid of Egypt, and there is another which has a striking resemblance to the Sphinx. Now the green hills in front of us appear to be climbing over one another like a troop of giants playing leapfrog, and there farther on they rise upward in cathedrals and forts of green a thousand feet high.

Now the sun comes out. It has penetrated that deep gorge in the mountains and turned the black water to silver. It catches the snow which is dusted over the green on the hills, and they are spangled with diamonds. It has caught the ice of that glacier and made it an immense lump of sapphire ice set in silvery snow.

Now the clouds are settling down upon the channel and hiding the sun. See, there is a wall of them in front of it. We are sailing into a snowstorm. A half-hour later we shall sail out into the sun again.

How the sky changes! Now it is blue overhead, with fleecy white clouds scattered here and there through it. See those cloud masses nestling in the velvety laps of the hills and wrapping themselves about the snowy peaks as though to warm them. Now the clouds seem to rise from the water, making a wall across the channel as high as our ship. Now they come down from the top, and we sail out of the dry air into a mist so thick that we can almost wash our hands in it as we go through.

Again we are out of the clouds. The air is clear. The sun is bathing the hills with its rays. The ferns, moss, and trees shine out in their green luxuriance, and the many cascades, some as big as your wrist and others no larger than your little finger, which fall down them, are threads and cords and ropes of silver.

These waterfalls come from the glaciers and the mountain snows.

Is it not strange that moss and green trees can grow so luxuriantly amid such surroundings? Yes; but it is only on the highest peaks that it is all snow and ice. Those trees are evergreens, and they are so close together that if we should land we might walk on their tops with snowshoes. A bed of moss, waist deep, grows among them, and great ferns with leaves as long as your arms extend out and cover every bare, rocky spot.

The glaciers which are found on the higher mountains extend down into the green, and now and then icebergs break off and fill up the channels. During some years this voyage is not possible, and, as it is, we make our way a part of the journey through fields of glacial ice. It is not like the ice of our rivers and lakes. It is as clear as crystal, and green rather than white.

There is a little iceberg now in front of the ship. It is not bigger than a city lot, and it does not extend out of the water so high as the deck. It is beautifully green, and as the sun catches it it looks like a great emerald rock with a top of frosted silver.

But the machinery is stopping! What is the matter? The captain tells us he is going to get some ice from that berg for the ship. The sailors are already bending over the rails. One of them has a long rope in his hands, with a running noose at its end. Now he gives it a throw. The coil flies out, and the noose catches on a projection of one corner of the iceberg. We have heard of lassoing cattle, but we have never heard of lassoing an iceberg before. Is it not strange? Yes, but not such a bad way after all. The other end of the rope is fastened to a wheel on deck moved by our steam engine, and as the wheel turns the rope is rolled up and the iceberg dragged close to the ship.

Now the steward and some of the sailors have taken one of the ship's boats and landed upon it. They are breaking off great lumps of ice with crowbars. They wrap chains about the ice blocks, and by means of a derrick the machinery of the steamer raises the blocks to the deck. Some of the blocks weigh many tons, and altogether we have got enough ice to last us for the rest of the voyage.

But what are those queer-looking boats which are making out from the shore? They look like canoes, and each has a fire in its center, about which huddle brown-skinned, frowzy-headed men, women, and children, almost naked. That man who is paddling the front boat wears little more than a vest, and that boat behind contains several children who have on no clothes at all.

"Each has a fire in its center."

These people are some of the savages who live in these waters along the coast of western Patagonia. They are called Alacalufes (ä-lä-kä-loo′fes). They are not like the Indians we have in America. They usually live in their canoes, although they sometimes sleep upon land in little wigwams about as high as your waist. They make the wigwams by bending over the branches of small trees and tying them together. They then build a fire in front, and crawl into their little houses for the night.

They seldom sleep in the same place for more than a week at a time, for it is much easier to build a new house than to go back home if they have wandered very far off.

The men have bows and arrows to defend themselves. The women, as a rule, do the fishing, using lines without

Alacalufes.

hooks. A little chunk of meat is tied to the end of the line, and when the fish has swallowed it the woman jerks it into her canoe.

Their food consists of fish, mussels, and now and then a fox, a seal, or an otter. They are fond of whale meat, and if they can find a dead whale they will feast upon it for weeks. They do not seem to care to have the meat fresh, for they cut it in pieces and bury it, digging it up for food as long as it lasts. They are fond of tobacco and biscuits, and row about our ship, holding out their hands and calling out in shrill voices, "Galleta! Galleta!" "Tabaco! Tabaco!" the two Spanish words for cake and tobacco.

As we look we wonder that they do not take cold. The hills on the shore are covered with snow, and we have on our heaviest clothing. There is not enough cloth in the whole crowd below us to make a full suit for a four-year-old child. We pity the poor naked savages, and one of us goes to his cabin and gets out a pair of old trousers. He throws them down into one of the boats. See, that woman has grabbed them. She evidently does not know what they are for, as she is tying them around her neck, fastening the legs over the chest. Until white people came here these savages used no clothes at all. A thick coat of whale oil or seal oil was enough to keep out the cold. Now they sometimes wear such cast-off things as they can get from the steamers, but as a rule they go naked.

The Alacalufes do not know the use of money. We try to buy some skins of them, and they sneer and draw back at the sight of our silver dollars and bank notes. They act differently as we show them some bright cloths and beads, and when the steward holds up a butcher knife one of the savages is glad to give him two skins in exchange. We ask them to come on board, but they are afraid and draw back. They are not friendly to strangers, and would kill a white man if they could catch one alone.

We see more savages on our way farther south. We cast anchor night after night, for it is too dangerous to travel by dark. The scenery grows grander and grander, until at last we steam through a narrow channel the mouth of which seems to be blocked by a great island. As we come nearer we see that there is a wide waterway beyond, and the captain tells us the island is called Desolation Island, and that we are at last in the Strait of Magellan.

Strait of Magellan.

Standing upon the deck as our ship turns to the east, we look back, and away off in the distance see massive rocks. They belong to Cape Pilar, at the entrance to the strait from the Pacific. In front of us the strait extends for a distance of more than three hundred miles, winding its way in and out between the mainland of Patagonia and the islands of the archipelago of Tierra del Fuego, until it opens out into the Atlantic.

Its scenery, however, is not so grand as that of Smythes Channel. In passing through the strait we are at times within a stone's throw of the shore. We sail under great mountains, and often in the distance see the high peaks of Tierra del Fuego, and of others of the islands of the archipelago. At the eastern end the channel is wider. The land is low, and the waters almost bound the horizon.

The Strait of Magellan is one of the commercial highways of the world. It was discovered in 1520 by a Spanish navigator, Ferdinand Magellan, and has been explored by other navigators from time to time.

For many years, however, the regions about it were little known, and for a time some supposed that Tierra del Fuego belonged to another continent which extended farther to the south.

The strait is about three hundred and fifty miles long, and it varies in width from two to twenty-four miles. It has deep waters all the way through, but it winds about so that large sailing vessels, on account of the winds, prefer to go about stormy Cape Horn, although this takes them many hundred miles out of their way.

It is different with steamers. They can move as well in the calms as when the wind blows. All steamers crossing the Atlantic between Australia and Europe, and those going to and from the east and west coasts of South America, pass through the strait. There are indeed so many ships that a city has grown up there on the tail end of the continent to furnish them coal and other supplies. This city is about midway through the strait. It is called Punta Arenas, or Sandy Point, and here we shall stay for a time.

XXI. AT THE END OF THE CONTINENT.

PUNTA ARENAS is the southernmost city of the world. It is so far along on the other side of the globe that people who live near our Canadian border would have to travel a distance as great as the diameter of the earth to get to it. It is at the very end of the continent, a thousand miles nearer the south pole than Cape Town, and several thousand miles farther south than any city of Europe or Asia.

It is a lonesome city. There is no town of any size within a thousand miles of it, and its supplies are brought to it by steamers. Great stores of coal and other goods are kept in Punta Arenas, for the ships passing through the strait often stop here to lay in a new stock of coal and other things for the long voyages which they have yet to make.

Punta Arenas.

We find English and German ships in the harbor, and there is a great steamer from New Zealand at anchor, with lighters beside her, and men loading and unloading freight.

We step out of our boat upon a pier, and by a short walk are in the heart of the city. What a queer place it is! It consists of scattered buildings built on the sides of the hills surrounding the harbor.

It has been cut out of the forest, and it reminds us of the frontier towns of our wooded Northwest. See the stumps in that vacant lot over there, and look at those trees on the hills at the back. Keep to the sidewalks. The streets are a mass of black mud, with here and there a puddle of water. See that team of oxen dragging its heavy cart through the mud. The wheels have sunk in to their hubs, and the eyes of the oxen almost pop out as they try to pull them on by the yokes tied to their horns.

What queer-looking houses! Few of them are of more than one story, and all have iron roofs. Many of the walls are made of sheets of galvanized iron; others are of logs or boards. It is only in the business parts of the city that there is stone or brick. None of the smaller buildings have chimneys. Those stovepipes sticking out of the windows, with elbows upturned, take their places.

Police Station, Punta Arenas.

What is that long, low structure of galvanized iron whose walls are wrinkled up like a washboard? There are soldiers in front, with swords at their sides. That is the police station. Those soldiers are under the governor of the territory of the Magellans, who lives in a big house on the other side of the square. He is appointed by the president of Chile, and has charge of this city, of the greater part of Tierra del Fuego, and of the thousands of islands of these far-away seas.

But what kind of people live away down here at this tail end of creation? We can learn from the men we see standing in knots on the corners of the streets or passing us as we go through the city. The most of them have their trousers tucked into their boots. They are roughly dressed. Many have long beards, and there are some we would not like to meet after dark.

They come from all parts of the world. They are talking together in German, Spanish, Italian, and Russian, and we often hear them speaking English and French. Here come two who are chatting in English. We hear the words "sheep" and "sheep farming." This is one of the chief sheep raising parts of South America, and the men in high boots are shepherds who have come to Punta Arenas to purchase supplies. Some live far north in Patagonia, and others have come from the sheep farms in Tierra del Fuego, across the strait.

As we go through the business part of the city we see that there are also many persons well dressed. The stores are quite large, and we learn that Punta Arenas has a big trade. Some of its houses are comfortable. It has a theater, churches, and schools, and we are surprised at the modern improvements which exist in this almost unknown part of the globe.

But we must not leave the Magellans without making a tour through the great archipelago south of the strait. It is composed of thousands of wooded islands which look very small on the map. Many of them are small, but all together they contain as much land as Kansas, and several are quite large, Tierra del Fuego proper being as large as Ohio. It lies just across the strait from Punta Arenas. There is a tugboat which goes there three times a week, and upon it we take passage for Port Venir (ve-neer'), a little town where the Chilean authorities on the island live. From here we make excursions by boat and land about this curious country.

The island of Tierra del Fuego has a rim of mountains around the greater part of it. The mountains rise in many places almost precipitously from the water, and upon them great glaciers hang down, now and then breaking off and falling into the sea with a terrible noise. The scenery is even grander than that of the strait, but the waters are often rough, and we have to move about very slowly.

At some places we see men washing the sands on the shore for gold. There are gold ledges in some parts of Tierra del Fuego which run far out into the sea. Here in time of storms the gold dust and nuggets are often thrown up on the beach. The miners go out as far as they can at low tide and gather up the sand, looking carefully over it for gold. Some of the gold is found in lumps as big as marrowfat peas. The precious metal, however, is difficult to get, and the men often work a long time in vain.

But let us go inland and see something of the interior of Tierra del Fuego. What a rich vegetation there is everywhere! We thought it was all snow and ice. We imagined it must be the bleakest part of the globe. It is, however, far different. It is only on the tops of the mountains that the snow remains all the year round, and the glaciers which move down their slopes are often bedded in green. The mountain slopes, for a thousand feet up from the water, are covered with trees, ferns, and moss so thick that we can hardly crawl through them.

How big the trees are! Some of the beeches are as tall as an eight-story building, and six feet in thickness. There are great magnolia trees and other trees somewhat like those of our central states. Nearly all of the trees are of the evergreen variety, and both trees and grass are green here the year round.

Over the mountains there are great plains of rich grass, which in the summer are spotted with wild flowers. There are wild gooseberries and wild raspberries. Wild strawberries of large size are found in their season, and there are also wild grapes and wild celery. The sheep farmers raise cabbages, potatoes, turnips, and peas in their gardens, and the pastures are so good that the sheep quickly grow fat.

We make our way inland to visit the sheep farms. The country in places is swampy and boggy, and as we ride on our horses over the plains we go very slowly because of the rats. The ground rats are one of the great pests of this region. They burrow through the earth, filling it with holes like a prairie dog town. They eat so much grass that the shepherds are anxious to destroy them. They do this by driving herds of cattle over the plains, which trample the rats to death.

We find that the sheep are kept in flocks of one and two thousand. Each flock is allotted a piece of land about as large as one of our townships, and it is watched by its own shepherd on horseback.

The shepherd has dogs to help him. Most of the dogs are Scotch collies, which are very intelligent. They understand their masters almost as well as though they understood language. When the shepherd makes a

motion to the front, they run ahead; if he motions to
the rear, they come back; and when he raises his hand in
the air, they stop short. Other motions will send them to
the right and left, and, in fact, as we see them driving the
sheep this way and that in response to their master's
orders, we think that human beings could not do better.

The shepherds do not feed the sheep. It is their business to see that they do not get lost, to keep off the panthers and Indians, and to look out for the vultures. The
sheep are so fat and heavy that when they fall down and
roll over on their backs they cannot get up. They lie there
kicking. The vultures of Tierra del Fuego are very cunning birds, and when they see a sheep in this helpless condition, they swoop down upon him and pick out his eyes.
The poor sheep is now blind. The vultures keep picking
at him, and he soon dies. They now quickly tear off the
skin and pick every bit of meat from the bones. It is the
shepherd's duty to be on hand when a sheep falls and to
help him to his feet again, and also to get him out of the
bogs if he should fall in.

Another great danger is from the Indians. Tierra del
Fuego contains some fierce savages called Onas, who wage
war with the shepherds and kill them whenever they can.
They steal in at night and drive off the sheep in flocks of
five hundred or more, and when they get them far away
in the forests they have a big feast. The Indian bands
are not large, and of course they cannot eat so many sheep
at a time. They kill what are left over, however, and bury
them in some deep stream or in the ground, leaving them
there until the chase of the shepherds is over, when they
go back and eat the decayed flesh.

Are not these curious Indians? Yes; and, strange to
say, they are among the finest-looking of the Indians of our

hemisphere. The men are usually about six feet tall, and the women are of about the same height as our women. The Onas have high cheekbones, flat noses, and dark eyes. Their hair is black and straight. The men singe their heads close at the crown, and the women let their hair grow so that it hangs down over their shoulders.

Onas.

The Ona Indians wear but little clothing, except loose skins which they wrap about their bodies. They live chiefly on the land, but do not like to stay more than a night or two in the same place, for they have an idea that the evil spirit is after them, and that they must move on or he will catch them. So they have no fixed homes. When they stop, they merely make a hole in the ground about three feet deep and weave branches over it. Here at night they crawl in and cuddle together, with their dogs about them for warmth.

The chief weapons of the Onas are bows and arrows, and they get their food by hunting and trapping.

Before we leave Tierra del Fuego we visit another tribe of Indians, which has now become partially civilized. This tribe is the Yaghan (yä′gan), which is largely confined to the southern part of Tierra del Fuego. Its people are much like the Onas, except that they are smaller. They get their living from the sea rather than from the land.

The Yaghans eat mollusks, fish, birds, and fungi. They cook birds by putting red-hot stones inside of them and then placing the birds on the coals. They have an odd way of roasting eggs. They break a hole in one end of the egg and stand it upright in the ashes before the fire, turning it round and round to make it cook evenly.

They are very good hunters, and the women are excellent fishers, being more fearless in the management of their boats and in swimming than the men.

XXII. IN ARGENTINA—PATAGONIA.

THIS morning we are again in Punta Arenas, ready to start up the eastern side of the continent. We shall make our way north through Patagonia, and for the next few weeks shall be traveling in Argentina.

Argentina is one of the richest and most healthful countries of South America. It has a vast territory. It is greater than the combined areas of our States east of the Mississippi river. It is twelve times as large as Great

Britain. It extends a long distance from north to south, having many different climates and products. In the north sugar cane, cocoanuts, and oranges grow; in the central provinces are wheatfields and rich pastures; while in the far south the country is almost altogether a sandy desert, with a climate somewhat like that of southern California.

The most of the country is flat. It is composed of great plains called pampas, upon which we may travel hundreds of miles without seeing a hill. There are only a few low mountain ranges. The most of the land is covered with pasture. On the western side of the country are the lofty Andes, which we saw in Chile.

Only a small part of the country is settled. There are now many more people in the State of New York than in Argentina. The population, however, is rapidly increasing. Immigrants are coming in from Europe to work in the cities or to raise wheat, cattle, and sheep in the country. So many people have come that every third man is a foreigner. The most of the immigrants are from southern Europe. They have come chiefly from Italy and Spain, although there are a few English, Germans, and French. We shall find the people far different from those of the west coast. There are not so many Indians, and there are many Italians.

Our first tour is to be over the rough lands of the far south. A coasting ship takes us from Punta Arenas out through the east end of the Strait of Magellan. We round Cape Virgin, on the northern side of the strait, and make our way along the coast, calling at the ports of Patagonia, and now and then stopping for a short run into the interior.

How bleak and bare everything is! The whole country seems to be nothing but sand. The only green spot is where we stop at the mouth of the river Chubut to visit a colony of Welsh shepherds who have come there to live. They have irrigated the land along the river and have rich crops of wheat.

Now we are again on the sea, going north, and now we sail up the deep but narrow harbor of Bahia Blanca (bä-hē'ä blän'cä), on the edge of a more fertile part of the country.

Bahia Blanca is the chief port of Argentina on the Atlantic. Buenos Aires, it is true, is a much larger city, but it is on the Rio de la Plata, two hundred miles inland from the ocean. Bahia Blanca is right on the sea. It has a good harbor, and the town which has grown up here is now accessible to all parts of the country by railroad.

A railroad has been built from it across the desert pampas to the foot of the Andes. It will soon go over the Andes through a low pass, and then crossing Chile will end at the port of Valdivia, on the Pacific. This will make a much shorter route from ocean to ocean than the Transandine Railroad farther north.

Let us take the new railroad and ride over the pampas to the foot of the Andes, stopping now and then on the way. What a curious region it is! We go for miles seeing nothing but sand, with thorny, scrubby bushes growing up here and there. There is little grass—so little, indeed, that it takes from three to five acres to furnish food for one sheep.

How wild everything is! There is not a fence to be seen. There are no barns, no roads, no farms, not anything living. There is nothing but thorn bushes and sand.

But stop. What are those yellow animals which are galloping away to the right? There must be fifty of them. They look like miniature camels. They are bigger than sheep and more beautiful than llamas. See how queerly they run. Their gait is more like short jumps than a gallop. What are they? They are guanacos, animals of the same family as the llamas, only wild and not quite so large. They are often hunted, but are hard to shoot. Our guide tells us that they have a keen sense of smell and that they can scent a hunter a full mile away. Their flesh, he says, is very good eating. It tastes much like venison, and when roasted over the coals is delicious. The fur is of a tawny yellow color spotted with white, and three or four skins sewed together make a beautiful rug.

Now we have left the guanacos far in the rear. We are again surrounded by nothing but thorn bushes and sand, with spots of white far off to the right. The white spots are moving. They are sheep, and that little brown thing which runs here and there through them is their shepherd on horseback. He is so far off that he looks like a pygmy, and his horse seems the size of a dog.

But what are those gray birds swimming through the air over the sand? They are coming toward us. That is a flock of ostriches with outstretched wings. They hold their heads far in front, and they fairly skim over the ground, their long legs kicking up a dust as they go. Some of them run very fast. There is one which has started up out of the bushes and is racing the train. We are going at a speed of forty miles an hour. The ostrich keeps up with us for a few minutes and then drops behind.

There are wild ostriches through this whole region, and had we time we might capture one. The proper way to catch ostriches is by means of the bolas. This is a long string of tough leather, with an iron ball as big as your fist at each end. The hunter rides after the ostriches on horseback, and when he gets near them he throws the bolas so that the string wraps itself around the legs of the ostrich, which falls to the ground.

Ostriches are not easy to catch. When hunted they often squat down and hide their heads in the sand. Many people who have not seen these birds in their homes think this foolish, but indeed on the desert there could be nothing more cunning. The feathers of the ostrich

"Ostriches are not easy to catch."

are of about the same color as the bushes of the pampas, and when one of them squats down and hides his head in this way he looks for all the world like a bunch of gray bush, and the hunter may ride by him without seeing anything strange.

The ostriches of the pampas are not those which furnish the feathers our mothers use in their bonnets. They are much smaller, and their feathers are coarser. These feathers are used to make feather dusters, and sometimes for feather rugs. The rugs are made of the breasts of the young birds, and it would be fine, would it not, if we could each take a rug of ostrich breasts home?

But here we are at a station. What a lonesome place for a town, and what a town! The half-dozen houses are gray one-story structures built of sheet iron. The station itself is of iron, and that water tank there stands upon a framework of iron.

The men on the platform are fierce-looking fellows with bright-colored ponchos over their shoulders. They all

"But here we are at a station."

carry knives, and we are told that they are gauchos, or cowboys, who herd the cattle and now and then work for the sheep farmers at shearing time. We shall see more of them as we go farther north.

Now we are again out on the desert. We have left the cars for a time and are alone on plains as dry as the coast of Peru. Our cheeks burn and our lips crack under the hot sun in the clear, thirsty air.

What is that cloud coming up? That surely is the sign of a storm. Hear the wind. It is blowing with the force of a blizzard and driving the cloud toward us. Yes, this is a storm, but not a rainstorm. That cloud is now between us and the sun. The sun is a great round red ball instead of the fiery white furnace it was a moment ago. The cloud is not vapor. It is dust and sand. We are in the midst of one of the sand storms of the pampas. Our guide drags us down into a hole he finds in the desert, and draws our blankets over the top.

Soon the storm is upon us. The sand comes down like fine hail. It sifts through the blankets, and we close our eyes. Now it is over, and we find we have a heavy load to raise when we push back the blankets. How queer we all look! We thought we were white, but the sand which has drifted through the blankets has turned us all brown. Our nostrils, ears, and mouths are filled with dust, and our clothes are covered with sand.

Such storms are common on the pampas of Patagonia. The dust comes in great clouds, and in the cities it covers the houses. It is as fine as flour, and closed doors and windows will not protect a house from it. It creeps through every crack and crevice, and covers everything with dust. Such a storm is much like a thunderstorm at home. The dust goes with the wind, and it is often followed by a drenching rain. This wets the dust in the air, and for a time it really rains mud. If the rain does not last long the houses are covered with mud, and it is only when the rain is heavy that they are scoured clean. These storms sometimes stop the railroad trains, so that it takes dust plows and men to clear off the track.

XXIII. IN ARGENTINA—LIFE ON THE PAMPAS.

A LONG ride by train has brought us back to Bahia Blanca. Here we again take the railroad, and are soon traveling through some of the great pasture lands of the world. Some parts of the country are fenced with barbed wire, but the most of it is just as nature made it —vast pampas which extend on and on until they lose themselves in the sky.

Now we see a flock of two thousand sheep browsing on the rich grass. Their white wool shines out among the dark-green bushes. We hear the shrill baa, baa, baa, of the lambs and the coarser voices of the old sheep as we go by.

Over there on the horizon is a drove of horses, mere brown specks against the blue sky, and between us and them a long train of huge carts, each hauled by eight oxen, is dragging its weary way over the plain. Those carts are filled with wool and hides, and the men who are walking beside them are driving the loads to the station.

In these pastures is found the chief wealth of Argentina. We might travel thousands of miles back and forth over the country and, with the exception of the rude huts of the herdsmen and now and then the larger buildings of some rich farmer, we should see little else than great flocks of sheep and droves of cattle and horses.

Argentina has tens of millions of sheep. Sheep raising is by far its most important industry. It has indeed so many sheep that if they were all divided equally each man, woman, and child in the country would have at least

LIFE ON THE PAMPAS.

"— vast pampas which extend on and on until they lose themselves in the sky."

twenty-five. The sheep are kept in large flocks and are watched by shepherds on horseback. They feed out of doors the year round, for there is good grass here in all seasons.

We see neither barns nor haystacks as we ride over the pampas. The inhabitants, as a rule, do not raise hay or corn for their stock. It is only necessary to let the animals graze, to protect the sheep from the vultures, and to give them a bit of salt now and then.

The sheep are shorn once every year. The wool is cut off and tied up in bales much as we bale cotton. It usually goes first to Buenos Aires, where it is transferred to the steamers and sent across the Atlantic to Europe.

Very few sheep are sold here for mutton. They are so plentiful that there is no great demand for their meat, and in the cities you can buy chops for four cents a pound. Within a few years, however, factories have been built to freeze mutton for shipment to Europe, where it will sell for from three to five times as much. In these factories the sheep are killed and dressed just as they are for our markets. They are then hung up in rooms which by certain chemical processes are made so cold that the meat soon freezes stiff. In this state it will keep fresh. It is now wrapped up in white cloths and carried to the refrigerators of the steamers which take it to Europe. As soon as it lands there it is thawed out and placed on the butchers' counters for sale. It then looks just like freshly killed mutton, and indeed it is said that when cooked it tastes like fresh mutton.

But let us leave the train and ride on horseback over the pampas. Here we are at the home of a shepherd. What a rude hut it is! Its walls are poles covered with mud, and its roof is straw thatch. We have to stoop as we enter the door, and we look about in vain for chairs for our party. The hut is scantily furnished. Much of the cooking is done on the ground outside. The oven is that round mound of mud which looks like a beehive.

The shepherd is an Italian. He lives with his little family all alone here, away out on the plain. He spends his day riding about among the sheep, and at night drives them into that corral near the hut. He works for a rich farmer who owns thousands of acres of land and more than one hundred thousand sheep.

The shepherd tells us that the estate, or estancia, is so large that we might ride all day in one direction and not come to its end. We learn later on that much of the land of Argentina is in large tracts. Land is not sold by the acre, but by the square league, which contains more than six thousand acres.

But suppose we go farther on over the pampas. We gallop for miles, now riding where the turf is soft, fresh, and green, and now where the grass is gray, dead, and coarse.

This is the natural grass of the pampas. The green turf has been pastured year after year. When so used the coarse grass disappears after a time, and a more tender and a richer grass springs up.

But see that smoke away off to the right. The flames are rolling up from the earth, and the dense white smoke is blowing toward us. Is that a prairie fire down here on the pampas? Don't be alarmed. There is no danger.

"Now they have caught one with a lasso."

The men who have lighted the fire have burned a strip around their fields so that it will not go beyond them. They are burning off the coarse grass and thorn bushes. After such a burning a more tender vegetation springs up. The owners say it makes the land better to burn off the grass once every few years.

But we have now left the sheep farm and are passing

through a large estate devoted to stock raising. We might ride eighty miles in a straight line and not get across it. It has great droves of cattle, and we pass herds of thousands of horses. There is one now where they are branding the animals. They have driven the horses into an inclosure fenced round by stakes. Now they have caught one with a lasso. See, they are driving him about in a circle. Now he is tired, and they pull him down to the ground. One man sits on his head, and another holds him tight by a rope fastened about his front leg, while a third seizes a red-hot iron from a fire near by and burns a mark on his side. That brand is the brand of the owner, and by it he can claim the horse if it gets lost.

Drying Horse Hides.

In that inclosure farther over, they are killing horses and skinning them. There are hundreds of fresh horse hides tied to stakes out there in the sun. They are stretched out to dry. In Argentina horses are raised largely for their hides. The animals are so cheap that you can buy one for a very few dollars.

It is not uncommon here for a man to give a horse to his friend. Even the poor natives own one or more horses. Indeed, it is said that a beggar sometimes follows his trade going from one farm to another riding upon his own horse, so that there really is a country where beggars go on horseback.

But look at those strange men who are branding the horses. They are dark-faced,

A Gaucho.

and they seem to be very fierce. What a queer dress they have! They do not wear trousers, but have blankets wrapped around their waists, the ends being tucked through between the legs and fastened to their belts. See, there is one standing at the side looking on. He has white drawers which extend down below his blanket and are edged with lace. Many of the others wear slouch hats. Each carries a whip, and all have knives in their belts.

Those are the gauchos, or, as we might call them, the cowboys of the pampas. They are the descendants of the Spaniards and Indians. They act as the herdsmen of the pampas. They do not like steady work, except such as can be done upon horseback, and they are always ready to ride over the plains to watch or drive cattle.

They are very good men when they are sober, but when drunk are by no means backward in using their knives. They are men of no education, and are not very civilized.

Gaucho Hut.

We enter one of their houses as we pass by on our ride over the pampas. We are in a mud hut fifteen feet square and so low that we have to stoop down to come through the door. The floor is of earth. Those dry bullock skulls scattered about are the seats, and a rude table, a box, and a chair comprise the rest of the furniture.

The cooking is done upon a fire outside the door. The food is usually beef, and it is roasted upon a spit over the coals. As the meat cooks, the gaucho's wife bastes it with the juice, which she catches in a pan as it falls.

After the meat is done it is cut off in large slices, being

usually eaten without plates or forks. Each one at the meal takes a slice in his hand. He puts one end of it between his teeth, and pulling out the slice as far as he can, he draws his knife across it within a sixteenth of an inch of his nose. When his first bite is chewed up he takes another in the same way, so that he really has no need of a fork.

A favorite dish is carne concuero (car′nā con-kwā′ro), or meat cooked in the skin. The meat is cut from the flesh of the animal, with the skin upon it. It is wrapped up tightly, so that the skin keeps in the juices when it is roasted over the coals. We try it ourselves and like it.

Cowboys at Breakfast.

XXIV. IN THE GREAT FRUIT AND BREAD LANDS OF SOUTH AMERICA.

WE shall travel to-day through some of the chief food lands of the world. Argentina has many different industries. It grows almost all kinds of crops, and we can describe only a few of them. We pass cattle and horses on our way back to the railroad, and see more sheep as we go on to the capital, Buenos Aires.

Here we change cars for the north, and ride for two days through the rich lands along the Parana river. We travel a long time by train through wheatfields and pastures. Every day the weather grows warmer, and at last we come into a land where there are oranges and lemons, and other tropical fruits. We are now in the province of Tucuman, in the northern part of the republic.

How different it is from the desert where we traveled after we left Punta Arenas! All nature is green, for the soil is rich and there is plenty of rain. We pass groves of tall palm trees, their green fanlike leaves rustling in the wind. We visit sugar plantations where gangs of men and women are cutting the cane. They chop it off close to the ground, and load it on ox carts to be hauled to the factory. We follow a cart and watch the cane stalks as they are thrown between steel rollers which squeeze out the juice, and farther on we see the juice boiled down into sugar.

We are now surrounded by mountains. There are streams everywhere. Some are almost dry now, for it is winter. In summer the rain comes down in great sheets and turns the streams to torrents. We can see how they

"Gangs of men and women are cutting the cane."

have cut deep gorges here and there through the hills. They often flood large tracts of land.

We see more hills as we leave Tucuman, going westward and southward through Argentina. The country is rolling. We are in the foothills of the Andes. There are forests of fine woods, and farther south we enter a land of great vineyards.

See how the vines cover the hills. They extend on and on for miles. The western part of Argentina is a rich wine raising country. Trainloads of grapes are shipped from here to Buenos Aires and to other parts of the republic. When the grapes are ripe, men, women, and children walk through the vineyards, gathering them in baskets and carrying them to the wine presses.

Look up at the mountains to the west. Those are the snowcapped Andes. This town we are coming into now is the little city of Mendoza, and that snowy peak just beyond is Aconcagua, which we saw in Chile. Mendoza is a station on the Transandine Railroad, and that iron

"We enter a land of great vineyards."

track which climbs up the mountains is the eastern part of the line which is to stretch from ocean to ocean, and over the western part of which we had such a pleasant journey in Chile some weeks ago.

There is a good railroad from here to Buenos Aires, and we can, in fact, travel by railroad to almost any part of the republic. We decide to go back to the wheat lands by the way of Cor'dova, and stop there for a few hours on the way.

Have you ever heard of Cordova? It is a town well known in the history of South America. It was for two hundred years one of the chief centers of education and culture on this continent, and it had a university seven years before our Pilgrim fathers landed on Plymouth Rock. Cordova has a large university now. It is also a business center, so that a stay in it will give us some idea of a small city in Argentina.

We take a carriage at the station and drive to the plaza. Cordova is much like the cities of Chile in that it is laid out in square blocks, with its streets crossing one another at right angles. The houses are almost all of one story. They are painted in the brightest of colors, and nearly all have iron bars over their windows, making us think of a jail.

Back of these bars we see women and girls standing or sitting. It seems to us as though the girls were caged in. This is so to a certain extent in all towns in Argentina. Young women and girls seldom go alone on the street. They are not allowed to associate with young men or boys until they are married, and a young man who should stop at a window and chat would be told he had better move on.

We drive on through the wide Avenida General Paz, admiring the statues at its ends, and then out among the shabby huts of the suburbs, where the poor people live.

Here all is dirty and squalid, but the sky is bright blue, and the gorgeous sunlight has given Cordova an atmosphere like that of the Orient. Its outskirts remind travelers of Cairo, and the Moorish architecture of the churches and the better class houses is like that of southern Spain.

Now we are again in the city. What queer names the streets have! Some are taken from the noted days of the history of Argentina. Here is one called Twenty-fifth of May Street. We turn the corner and go into the street of the Eighteenth of July, and wonder if we shall not find farther on a street named "Week after Next."

We stop at the market. It is in a hollow square surrounded by rose-colored one-story buildings containing the meat stalls. The red beef and mutton hang down from

"We stop at the market."

hooks under dirty white awnings. There are no scales. Those women with the black shawls around their heads, who are buying, pay for the meat by the chunk.

The market court is filled with carts which have come in from the farms. On the ground sit dark-faced women with vegetables about them, which they sell by the pile.

GREAT FRUIT AND BREAD LANDS.

What is that squealing outside the market? It sounds like a pig in the hands of a butcher. They surely cannot kill hogs here in the midst of the city. It is only the creaking of a farm cart which is bringing wheat to the market. There it comes through the door. It has wheels eight feet in height, with hubs as big around as your waist, and an axle as thick as a telegraph pole.

"It has wheels eight feet in height."

The cart has an arched cover of reeds over its bed. The skins which have been sewed to the top are put there to keep the rain off the wheat. Such farm carts take the place of farm wagons throughout Argentina. They look very rude, but each cart will hold several tons—so much, indeed, that teams of twelve oxen are often hitched to one cart. The owner of the cart is that dark-faced man in the poncho, and his wife is the woman in the calico dress who is now climbing out.

But let us leave Cordova and ride on the railroad into the wheat lands. We reach them within a few hours after leaving the city. The best wheat region of Argentina lies in the Parana basin, within a hundred miles of both banks of the river, for the soil which it has brought down from the uplands is exceedingly rich. The wheat lands are all together so large that if they could be put into one block they would make a wheatfield five times the size of New York, or six times that of Ohio. This tract in good seasons produces far more wheat than the people can use, and the wheat exports are sometimes so large that they compete with our wheat in the markets of Europe, and as a result we receive much lower prices.

Our farmers, indeed, might have to stop exporting wheat did not Argentina have many droughts, when the wheat will not grow, and also in good seasons terrible invasions of locusts which sometimes eat up the crops.

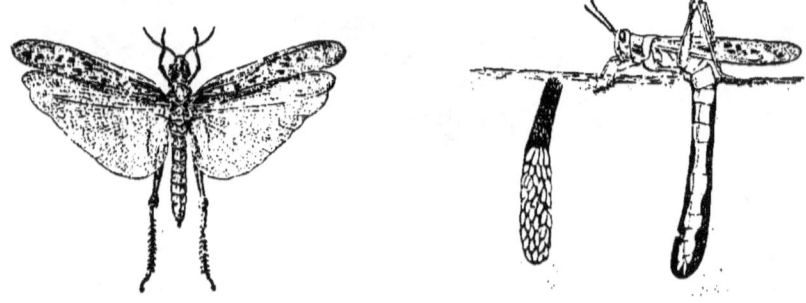

Locusts and Their Eggs.

The locusts come down in swarms of millions from the warm lands of southern Brazil. There are so many of them at times that they shut out the sunlight like a storm cloud. They alight on everything green and eat up all as they go. They eat the leaves of the trees and also the fruit. They are especially fond of green wheat. A swarm of them will chew up a wheatfield in a night, and when they come in vast numbers, as they sometimes do year after year, the crops of the farmers are ruined. They lay their eggs in the holes in the ground, and these hatch out thousands more. The people never know when they are coming, and plant on and on, hoping they may be able to harvest their crops.

We pity the farmers as we watch them at work. It is spring, and they are plowing the fields. We ride for hours through vast tracts of brown soil upon which dark-faced men are guiding their oxen this way and that through the furrows. Here one is sowing the seed, scattering it by hand over the land, and in the next field oxen are dragging harrows and brush over the clods to cover the grain.

Now we are passing farms where the wheat has been sown for some time. As far as we can see there is nothing but the emerald green of the fresh sprouting grain. A little later on, as harvest time comes, this vast sea of emerald will change to a billowy ocean of gold. There will be wheat on all sides, and the yellow waves will roll on and on until at last they lose themselves in the blue sky.

Then there will be reapers and mowers moving over the fields, some drawn by horses, some by oxen, cutting the grain. There will be steam thrashers puffing away as they shell the wheat out, and there will be great ox carts, like those we saw in the markets of Cordova, with teams of eight and twelve oxen hauling the great loads of bags to the train.

At that time, were we here, we might find it very slow traveling. There is so much wheat that all the freight cars of the country are needed to carry it to Rosario, the chief port of the Parana, and to Buenos Aires for shipment to Europe. The tracks are so crowded with wheat cars that the passenger trains are sometimes kept back to let them go by. We should then find stacks of bags awaiting shipment at the stations, many of the stacks being covered with canvas to protect the wheat from the rain.

Why do not the farmers store the wheat in barns? We can easily see as we ride on and on through the fields. There are no barns anywhere! No feed is stored, and the stock is seldom kept under cover. Even the working horses and oxen are turned out to graze. There are

"There will be steam thrashers puffing away."

no farm buildings except the little mud huts thatched with straw in which the small farmers live. The huts are so small that there is no place in them for storing wheat. The result is that the grain is sold as soon as it is thrashed, and the farmer must take what he can get.

Most of the grain is shipped to Europe soon after harvest. This is along in January and February, in the middle of our winter. There is so much wheat, however, that some is exported all the year round. We can see how it is handled by watching the loading of steamers at Rosario.

Rosario is one of the chief wheat ports of Argentina. It is situated on the south bank of the Parana river, about three hundred miles by water from Buenos Aires. It is of about the size of Indianapolis. It is built right on the banks of the river, which is here so deep that great ocean steamers can sail through the Rio de la Plata and the Parana up to it.

Rosario is built upon a bluff so high that it is above the masts of the steamers on the water below. All along, a little back of the edge of the bluff, warehouses of gray galvanized iron have been constructed. In these the wheat is stored as it is brought from the fields.

Loading a Steamer, Rosario.

Now, in front of each warehouse, there is a long chute, or trough, made of wood or iron, extending down to the water. These troughs are in sections, so that they can be shortened or lengthened at will, and so that when connected they make a continuous chute running from the bluff right into the hold of the steamer.

The bags of wheat are carried by men from the warehouses and thrown into the chute. Gravity makes them descend, and they bounce up and down as they fly into the steamer, making us think of an army of gigantic yellow mice galloping down into the hold. At some places the railroad tracks run close to the bluff, so that the wheat bags can be taken from the cars direct to the chutes.

XXV. IN BUENOS AIRES.

IT is a night's ride by train from Rosario to Buenos Aires. We go to bed in the sleeper as the cars move out of the station, and when we awake we are in the capital of Argentina. We step out into a railroad station, as large almost as our best stations at home, and walk under a long glass-covered roof to the front door. What a lot of carriages there are, and how their drivers yell at us in Spanish as we come down the steps! We choose one, and are soon dashing through one long street after another, turning corner after corner, until we reach our hotel.

As we go we see that Buenos Aires is a large city. Its size grows upon us as we ride through it day after day. It is indeed the largest city on the South American continent. It has already nearly a million inhabitants, and it increases in population, it is said, about one hundred thousand a year. It grows fast because it is the chief city of Argentina. It is situated on the Rio de la Plata, at just the point where steamers from Europe can most easily land their goods, and from where the wool, hides, meat, and other things raised here can be easily loaded to go across the ocean.

Buenos Aires is the place where the most important business of Argentina is done. It is the capital and has the principal officials. It has nearly all the factories that

Buenos Aires.

supply Argentina with goods. It ships most of the wool and other exports. Indeed, it is one of the largest produce markets in the world.

In Buenos Aires the richest of the people of Argentina live, only now and then going out to their vast estates in the country. Here also are the homes and business houses of the great merchants. Here are the chief colleges, the great daily newspapers, the finest churches, and, in fact, all things which are of supreme importance in Argentina.

But what kind of people live in this city? When we hear them talk we think them all Spanish. There are Spanish signs over the stores, and many of the people speak nothing else. Buenos Aires is by far the largest Spanish-speaking city of the world, being more than twice as large as Madrid, the largest city of Spain. Still, the most of its people are foreigners. Not more than one fifth of them were born in the country. There are more Italians in Buenos Aires than natives of Argentina, and there are at least one hundred thousand who have come here from Spain.

See that group of dark-faced men with ruddy complexions on the opposite corner. They wear short jackets and full skirts, and their trousers are held up by sashes tied

Basques.

about their waists. They have little round caps on their heads, and many of them carry long ropes. You might think they were hangmen, but even Buenos Aires could not give work for so many executioners. Those men are Basques. They come from northern Spain, and are here

Street Scene.

because they can find plenty of work and good wages. They are porters, and their ropes are to tie on the boxes or bags which they carry on their backs through the streets.

The masons who are building that house over the way are Italians. The Italians are the mechanics of the city, and we shall also find them peddling onions, fish, and all kinds of goods from house to house. They are the newsboys of Buenos Aires, and also the bootblacks. They own the grocery stores, and there are some rich Italian bankers and traders. There are many large banks managed by the English, and some of the biggest stores are owned by the Germans.

But let us go farther on into the business section. Here we are in the Plaza de Mayo. What a beautiful park, and how large are the houses about it! That great building on one side of the square is the cathedral. There is a crowd of women in black gowns, with black shawls over their heads, going to mass. The building covers more than an acre, and it will hold, it is said, nine thousand people. It is the chief church of the city; for Argentina is a Catholic country, and Buenos Aires is said to be the largest Catholic city of the world. Catholicism is the religion of the state, and it is at the cathedral that the president attends mass.

That building just above the cathedral contains the courts of the city, and on the opposite side is the government house, where the president of Argentina has his offices, and where the most of the government business is done. Argentina has a president and Congress just as we have, and its people are supposed to choose their own officers, although elections are often unfair.

But let us go out to Barraccas. "Barraccas" means warehouses, and this is the name of that part of the city where the most of the wool, wheat, and meat are prepared for shipment to Europe. We stand on the corner and wait for the car. We hear a horn blown in the distance. The sound of it grows louder and louder, and we soon see that one end of the horn is in the mouth of the car driver, and that he gives a blast as a warning at every street corner.

As the car stops we climb in. We are carried through narrow streets for more than two miles, when we reach an enormous brick building on the banks of the Riachuelo river, which here flows into the Rio de la Plata. The

"Some are filled with wool."

building is that of the Mercado Central des Frutos, the largest wholesale produce market, under one roof, in the world. It covers many acres, and in it millions of pounds of wool are handled each year. It is so built that the cars can come into the market, and the wool and wheat can be unloaded right upon the floors. Shiploads of wool sail up to its doors, and carts and wagons loaded with wool and grain are driven in from all parts of the country. We spend a long time going through one immense room after another. Some are filled with wool, and in others there are so many bags of wheat and corn that we have not time to count them.

On our way back we call at one of the big city markets. Here we see that the food which these people eat is quite as good as our own. They have all sorts of meats, fish, and vegetables. There are huge pears from near Buenos Aires, and oranges and pineapples which have come down on the steamer from Paraguay. There are grapes from the foothills of the Andes, and peaches by the bushel from the islands of the Parana river. Peach trees grow so rapidly in this part of the world that they are often raised for fuel, and there are so many peaches in some places that they are thrown to the pigs.

Chicken Peddler.

We stop at the stalls where chickens are sold. The feathers have been pulled from the chickens, except the tail feathers. These show what the color of each chicken was before it was plucked. Why these feathers are left I do not know. A similar custom prevails in South China, where dog meat is sold to be cooked. A bit of the dog's hair is always left on the tail; but this is because the Chinese think the flesh of black dogs the best and most fitted to put a brave spirit into the eater.

We meet many chicken peddlers on leaving the market. They are starting out with live chickens, which they will sell from house to house through the city. The chickens are in wicker crates hung over the back of a horse, and we see that all peddling is done by men on horseback or on foot.

Now and then we pass a peddler who is driving a flock of turkeys before him. The fowls are for sale. If you pick out one the peddler will catch it for you.

Have you ever eaten young armadillo? Its meat tastes like spring chicken, and the people of Argentina are so fond of it that they eat a thousand armadillos a month. The armadillo is a four-legged animal, with a shell like a turtle and a little head like a pig. It burrows in the earth, and seldom goes out of its hole except at night. It eats fruit and roots, and sometimes small insects. Its flesh is white and quite tender, and when we taste it at one of the restaurants we find it delicious.

Armadillo

But it is now five o'clock, and we must go for a walk on the Calle Florida. This is the fashionable shopping street of the city. It is lined with the stores of jewelers, confectioners, milliners, and tailors, and at this time of day the fashionable people come here to see and be seen.

The street is just wide enough for a line of carriages to move up one side of it while another line goes down the other. We find the Florida filled with carriages. There are hundreds of horses prancing along. There are fine carriages containing well-dressed women and men. The carriages drive slowly up and back, while the people within sit and stare at their neighbors.

Upon the sidewalks are knots of young men who have come here for their afternoon outing, to chat with one another and look at the crowd.

We see more fine turnouts on Thursday afternoon, when

we take a drive out by the magnificent residences along the Avenue Alvear to Palermo Park.

This park is perhaps the finest in all South America. It covers many acres, and in it there are long avenues of magnificent palms, forest trees of all kinds, running

Palermo Park.

streams, and winding lakes. During the afternoons of Sunday and Thursday it is filled with people. There are hundreds of carriages and thousands of foot passengers riding and walking under the palms. There are gayly dressed children playing upon the grass, and boys rowing about in boats upon the lakes.

XXVI. URUGUAY—IN MONTEVIDEO, THE PARIS OF SOUTH AMERICA.

WE begin our journeys in a new country this morning. We have left Buenos Aires, and after traveling all night on a great river steamer are now casting anchor in the harbor of Montevideo. The day is just dawning, and the lights on the shore shine out through the mist, marking the shape of the city and harbor.

The bay is like a horseshoe six miles in length and is so large that many hundreds of vessels could be anchored in it at one time. Of late years, however, the mud brought down from the highlands through the Rio de la Plata has so filled it up that the largest ships must now stay several miles from the shore.

We have to wait some time on the ship for the health officers and inspectors of customs. While we wait, let me give you a bird's-eye view of Uruguay. It is the smallest of the South American republics. There are single states in Argentina which surpass it in size, and it could easily be lost in Brazil. It is only about as large as Missouri. It has, all told, not more people than Boston.

We can see something of its shape on the map, but if we could fly over or perhaps ride above it on the winged horse Pegasus, we might know it much better. We should then see that, with the exception of a few low mountain ranges, the country is a waving sheet of billowy green, with so many streams of silvery water flowing through it that they make a network upon it like the veins of a leaf. We should see that it has rich soil, and that cattle and sheep are scattered over it in quite as large flocks as those of Argentina.

If we looked closely we might see that the houses of the farmers are like the mud huts we saw on the pampas, and that the aspects of nature are about the same.

The climate of Uruguay is delightful. The country is as near the equator as Florida is, but the weather is not so hot in the summer, nor so cold in the winter. The seasons are the opposite of ours, so that when we have autumn Uruguay has spring, and when we put on our furs the Uruguayan ladies are using their fans.

In such a flight we should notice the long coast line of the country, and might see great steamboats sailing up the Uruguay river, and smaller boats on other streams in the interior. We should see but few large towns, and should notice that all railroad trains, steamboats, and carts are moving to and from the capital, the city of Montevideo, which we are about to explore.

We take a boat and ride to the wharves, noticing as we go the Cerro, or hill, at the left, from which the city was named. Montevideo means " I see the mountain." The Cerro is the mountain. It is not quite so high as the Washington Monument, but the land is so flat all about it

Montevideo.

that from the sea it can readily be distinguished far off. There is a white tower upon it, and at night you can see the revolving light in it twenty-five miles out from land.

But here we are at the wharves. We step out and wend our way through the city. What large buildings are these all about us! They surpass those of any city we have yet seen on our tour. Montevideo is well built, and its people are proud of its great business blocks.

How clean the streets are! This comes from the long tongue of rock upon which Montevideo is built. The rock extends from the Cerro out into the bay. It slopes so on all sides that the streets are all up hill and down, and every rain washes them clean. Montevideo is a very healthful city, and fewer people die in it, in proportion to its size, than in any other city of the world.

"We take a boat and ride to the wharves."

Get out of the way of those carts! They are each drawn by two or three mules harnessed abreast. How huge and clumsy they look! Each cart has a bed made of poles; it has sides of poles curved upward and tied together with thongs. Look at the wheels. They are enormous. Hear the din they make as they rattle over the cobblestone streets. There are other carts coming up this side street. It is queer they do not use wagons. No; not when you learn that all vehicles in Montevideo are taxed by the number of wheels, and that a four-wheeled wagon would have to pay twice as much as a cart.

Montevideo has very good street cars. The streets of the city run so up hill and down that few cabs are used. We can go anywhere on the street cars. We ride upon them by two-story and three-story houses, now passing

"We visit the Solis Theater."

great plazas, or squares, filled with trees. We go out into the country, past beautiful houses with gardens about them, and come back to the city by a new line.

We visit the Solis Theater. It is one of the largest in South America, covering two acres and having seats for three thousand people. We go to the cathedral, and spend some time in visiting the national museum and the public libraries. Montevideo has a university. It has good common schools, and we learn that public schools are being established in all parts of the country. At present, however, only about one child in ten goes to school, and the most of the common people cannot read or write.

In the schools the children study out loud. We can tell by the din that a school is going on long before we come to the block in which it is.

Cathedral and Plaza.

Montevideo has many rich people who have vast estates throughout the country. They live upon these in the summer and spend their winters in their great houses in Montevideo. We stay some weeks in Uruguay and have opportunities to visit well-to-do families. Their houses are grand, but exceedingly cold. The floors are marble, and the ceilings are often upheld by marble columns imported from Italy. There are no fires, for the people believe artificial heat unhealthful, and so they do not have stoves, furnaces, or steam-heating pipes. The result is that when it is cold the women receive their callers sitting in their furs, with their feet on hot-water bottles, and the men often wear their overcoats when at the table for dinner.

Some of the queerest customs of these people are those of courtship and marriage. Young women and men cannot walk together by themselves, as they do in our country. Indeed, a Uruguay girl must never go out on the street unless she has her mother, her aunt, or a servant girl with her, and should her boy friends call they would meet the whole family.

When a young man begins to court a young woman he does not come into her house, but stands for days in front of the building, and stares at her window. In a short time she sees him staring. She at once knows what he means. Then perhaps she opens the window and stares in return.

The two are not supposed to talk to each other, but they stand thus staring for hours at a time. This is what is called in Montevideo "playing the dragon," the young man being the dragon. I will not say that never a wink nor a whisper passes between the two young people, but if so it must be while no one is looking. After a time the young man goes to the father of the young woman, and tells him he wishes to call at the house with a view to a proposal of marriage. If he gets the father's consent, he comes and spends the evening with his sweetheart and her family, getting her as far off from the rest as he can. He is not allowed to see her alone until they are married.

This custom seems odd to us, and we often slyly laugh in our sleeves when we see a young man dressed in his best parading up and down in front of a window. We do not dare to laugh openly, for this might make the young man angry, and if he became jealous we might have to fight him straightway.

From Montevideo we take some trips through the country. We visit the larger towns by railroad and travel some time on the Uruguay river. Here we see the great meat-extract establishments. The largest of them are at Fray Bentos, where hundreds of thousands of cattle are yearly killed for meat-extract. The lean meat is stewed in warm water, being skimmed again and again of the fat. After a long time the stew thickens into a liquid like thin molasses. When it cools, it thickens. It is now put up in tin boxes and sent to Hamburg, Germany, where it is repacked in little porcelain jars and shipped all over the world. Many of us have tasted beef tea made from this Uruguay meat. It is found in our drug stores, and is often prescribed by the doctors for sick people.

Not far from Fray Bentos we find factories in which dried or jerked beef is made. Such meat is much liked by the South American people, and is taken by the shipload from Uruguay to Brazil and the West India Islands. The animals are killed, and the meat is stripped from their bodies in sheets and dried in the sun in such a way that it will not spoil, however long it is kept.

XXVII. UP THE RIO DE LA PLATA SYSTEM INTO THE HEART OF SOUTH AMERICA.

WE are again upon shipboard this morning. We have left Montevideo and are steaming through the Rio de la Plata, upon whose tributaries we shall go into the heart of the South American continent.

What a big stream it is! At Montevideo we could hardly see the opposite shore. It is wide all the way to Buenos Aires, and it is many miles wide where it is formed by the junction of the Uruguay and Parana rivers, still farther up. The Rio de la Plata, in fact, is more like a muddy fresh-water bay or arm of the sea than a river. It is almost two hundred miles long, and where it unites with the ocean it is more than one hundred miles wide.

Rio de la Plata.

How muddy it is! The water looks like pea soup. It is so dirty that we hesitate to get into our bath, and when we let off the water a thick coat of mud remains in the tub. It is so thick that our feet leave marks in it as deep as those which so frightened Robinson Crusoe on the shore of the desert island. The Rio de la Plata brings down a vast amount of earth washings from the mountains. It contains so much that if it could all be put upon wagons twenty thousand horses all pulling at once could not haul away the load of one hour. So much mud drops to the bottom that the river is fast filling up. It is already difficult for the big ocean steamers to reach Buenos Aires, and the people are now talking of a system of jetties like that of the Mississippi to deepen the river.

The Rio de la Plata system drains a basin about half as large as the whole United States. If we could view it from above we should see that it is of the shape of a great horseshoe, with the opening toward the Atlantic. The highlands of Brazil and the Andes form the upper rim and back of the shoe, while the slightly sloping plains of Patagonia are the rim on the south. Within this shoe lie the best lands of Argentina, the whole of Uruguay and Paraguay, and large portions of Peru and Bolivia.

In climate this basin is like that of the Mississippi river basin reversed, the greatest tributaries of the system coming from the hot lands of Brazil and Bolivia, where palms and rubber trees grow, and its mouth lying in the cooler countries of wheatfields and pastures in which we have lately been traveling. Almost everywhere its climate is healthful. Its northern parts have weather much like that of Louisiana or Florida, and the south has much the same climate as our middle States. Our ship stops at Buenos Aires for passengers and freight, and we then start on our way to the great Parana.

We soon pass the mouth of the Uruguay river, and just before entering the Parana river we sail about the large island of Martin Gracia (grä-sē′ä). We can see with our glasses the fort upon its shore. There are boys in soldier uniforms marching about it. They belong to the Argentina Naval School, which has been established there, and the men who are drilling are soldiers used to defend the great fortifications. Martin Gracia is called the Gibraltar of Argentina, for it guards the chief entrance to the Parana river. It is one of the historic points of this region. It was here that the Spanish explorers who first visited Uruguay stopped for a time. During their stay their pilot, Martin Gracia, died, and they gave the island his name as a monument. As we sail by it we remember that we, too, are on an exploring expedition. We are entering waters which were discovered by the white man who, with his father John, was the first to set foot upon the soil of the North American continent. This was Sebastian Cabot, who, only thirty-four years after Columbus landed in America, came here and entered the Parana river. He traveled up that part of the Parana through which we shall go, and from it went into the Paraguay river over the very same way we shall sail.

I venture, however, that Sebastian Cabot, if he could be with us to-day, would think our boat more wonderful than anything he saw on his tour. His ship was not one tenth as large. It was a small sailing vessel, and it took months for it to go up the river. He would wonder how we could move without sails. Steam as a motive power was not then discovered, and he would not at first understand how we could make the great paddle wheels at the side of the ship move it onward so fast that the voyage can be made in six days.

Cabot's ship was probably lighted with oil or tallow. How he would wonder at our electric globes and the other curious things which have been invented since then!

He would probably stare when he sat down to dinner, and might think that our meals are rather good for explorers. Here, for instance, is our bill of fare for one dinner: ox-tail soup, Bologna sausage with potato salad, boiled beef, fish caught in the Parana river, curried chicken and rice, beefsteak and potatoes, cheese, guava jelly, English walnuts, almonds and raisins, oranges and coffee.

Passing Martin Gracia, we sail for several hundred miles through the delta of the Parana. The river for a day's ride north of its mouth is about twenty miles wide. It has

On the Parana.

many channels, and it is dotted with islands, some covered with forests of peach trees and others cultivated by the Italians, who raise vegetables for the Buenos Aires markets.

All of the islands are low, and many have curious houses upon them. We are passing some now. They look like sheds. They are raised upon piles, the first floor being reached by long ladders. This is that the people may keep out of the way of the floods, for the winds and the tides sometimes roll great waves in from the ocean.

After traveling for a day among such islands, we reach Rosario. We steam by the great ocean ships which we saw from the bluff after our tour of the wheatfields. They are still loading wheat, and thousands of yellow bags are bobbing up and down as they gallop over the chutes. There are big flour mills and grain elevators at

Santa Fé and other towns farther up, and much of the shipping of the Parana river is devoted to carrying grain.

As we go on we are more and more delighted. The Parana is picturesque, although the lowest parts of it have no very grand scenery. It is wider than the Mississippi. It seems at times like a great inland sea, the shores being so far apart that we cannot always see both banks at once.

This is largely due to the islands, of which the Parana has so many that they have never been counted. It probably has more islands than any other river of the world. In our journey we are always sailing in and out among them, now coming close to the high bluffs of the mainland, and now passing through narrow channels so near to the islands that we can almost catch hold of the willows and feathery grasses which hang over and mirror themselves in the water.

But some of the grassy islands are moving. That great mass of green over there is going past our steamer on its way down the river almost as fast as our engine is pushing us up the stream. See, the waves from the ship are making the island move up and down. It is a sheet of billowy green rising and falling with every wave. That is a floating island! There are many such in the Parana river. They are masses of weeds, flowers, and turf which the floods have torn from their foundations in the highlands and are carrying down to the sea. Some are so firm that they will support a man, and during the floods jaguars, snakes, and peccaries are carried upon them to the islands about Buenos Aires.

Now we have left the middle of the stream and are passing close to the great bluffs on the mainland. We are trying to keep away from that sand bar which is being built up by the river. In places the banks are being torn down, and we have all about us examples of how the waters aid in transforming the earth.

We can see that the rivers are indeed the masons of the gods, and as we look about us can realize what a master workman this mighty Parana is. The waters which are sweeping past us, going faster than a man can walk, are loaded with mud. They have been carrying down mud for ages, and those islands beyond us have been built up from the soil they have dropped.

The streams in the Andes are now gathering dirt for this river, and its waters are carrying it down to the lowlands. That island of a hundred acres of green over there is made of earth washings which have been brought from the highlands. Some of its particles were washed from the roots of palm trees in Brazil, some came from coffee plantations a thousand miles farther north, and some were perhaps loosened by the Indians we saw mining gold in the wilds of the Bolivian Andes. That bluff at our right is one hundred feet high. See how its earth strata, or layers, are piled up one on top of the other like those of a jelly cake. Those layers have been deposited there during the ages, and as we steam on we can see some of the lands of the future rising slowly under our eyes.

Notice that spot at the right of the vessel. I mean just over there where the water is rippling. That is a sand bar. Next month it will be a sandy island. Next year it will be covered with grass, and trees will sprout up, sending down, as they grow, their long, fibrous roots to hold in the soil. During every flood old Mother Parana will spread a new coat of soil over her island child, and soon will appear one of the forest-grown patches which dot the vast bed of the river.

Is not nature a wonderful thing? We realize it more

at every turn of the wheel. The land and the sky seem to change every hour, and the scenes above us are even more glorious than those below. The sunsets are gorgeous. They paint the clouds with all the hues of the rainbow, and make a golden canopy over the dark-blue Parana. We get up before day to see the sun rise. As it comes up its rays strike the dewdrops upon the feathery grasses of the islands, and myriads of diamonds flash from the emerald fields. At night both the heavens and the earth are clad in the glorious moonlight of the semi-tropics. We linger late upon deck, picking out the Southern Cross from among the stars, and wondering at the remarkable brilliancy of the Milky Way.

Corrientes.

As we travel on toward the equator we see many more trees; the islands are covered with them. The grasses are more luxuriant, and here and there are bunches of ferny bamboo. Now and then there is a palm tree shading a house on the mainland, and oranges and lemons are brought to the steamer at some of the ports. We stop at many small towns of one-story buildings with thatched huts about them. The houses are roofed with red tiles, and there is always a church spire rising high above the rest of the town.

After three days we reach the city of Corrien'tes. It is quite a large town for this part of the world. It has about thirty thousand people, and looks very imposing in its position on the high east bank of the Parana river. It is close to the junction of the Parana and the Paraguay rivers, and at its landing we see steamers starting up the Parana, upon which they can sail farther on to the northeast for hundreds of miles.

Our own ship, however, is on its way to Asuncion (ä-sōōn-sē-ōn'), in Paraguay, and as Paraguay is the country we are next to explore, we leave the Parana, and steam up the Paraguay river.

The water here is not so muddy as that through which we have been traveling. The stream is not so wide. It is, however, a mighty river, as deep as the Mississippi, and about eighteen hundred miles long. It is navigable for steamers for more than a thousand miles above Corrientes, and small boats can go upon it far into Brazil.

We get our first sight of Paraguay soon after we leave Corrientes. That land on the east bank belongs to it, and those villages with orange trees about them are filled with Paraguayan people.

As we sail onward we find the country wilder. Now and then we go for miles with virgin forests on both sides of us. The steamer moves this way and that in following the channel, and we are often close to the banks. We hear parrots screaming at us from the woods, and with the glass we now and then catch sight of a monkey grinning out of the leaves of a tree. There are birds of beautiful plumage, and a flock of wild ducks now and then rises from the lagoons which we pass at every few miles.

Landing at Asuncion.

We get out our guns and take a shot at the birds. We shoot at the alligators on the shore, and now and then one scuds through the water to swim out of the way of the boat, diving down as we pass.

The west bank of the river is especially wild. This is a part of a vast wilderness known as the Chaco, the lower part of which belongs to Argentina, and the upper to Paraguay. In the Chaco there are miles and miles of virgin forest. The most of it is inhabited by savages, and we are told that we could not travel a mile from the banks of the river without meeting jaguars, monkeys, and wild hogs.

We stop now and then at a Paraguayan town, and finally land at the wharves of Asuncion, the capital of Paraguay.

XXVIII. IN PARAGUAY.

PARAGUAY lies about as far inland from the Atlantic Ocean as the State of Illinois, but by our winding way up the rivers we have journeyed as great a distance as from New York to Omaha. We are now about midway on the west border of Paraguay proper, and just opposite the lower corner of a vast wilderness known as the Paraguayan Chaco.

Paraguay is composed of two divisions, Paraguay proper and the Chaco. Paraguay proper corresponds to our States. The Chaco is more like our Territories. It is the "wild west" of Paraguay. It is inhabited only by savage Indians and wild beasts. It is a vast territory lying west of the Paraguay river and north of the Pilcomayo river, being bounded on the north by Bolivia. The Chaco has large forests, extensive swamps, and some good lands. It is almost all in a state of nature, having been little explored.

Paraguay proper is the settled part of the country. It has all the cities and towns, and is the only part in which civilized people live. It lies east of the Paraguay river and north of the Parana river, being located somewhat as Illinois is in our own country, the Parana corresponding to the Ohio river, and the Paraguay to the Mississippi.

Paraguay proper is about as large as Illinois, and it is much like it in character. The country is beautifully rolling, with numerous streams upon which the crops can be moved to the ports of the Parana and Paraguay rivers. It has great pastures and large tracts of rich soil. There are one or two low mountain ranges running through the country. These mountains are covered with forests, and they add greatly to the beauty of the scenery.

The climate and products are semitropical. There are small plantations of tobacco, manioc, and sugar cane. There are orange trees everywhere, and clumps of palm trees upon the great plains.

The people of Paraguay are few. They are composed of the whites, of the mixed race, and of pure Indians. Those of the white and mixed races number only about six hundred thousand, and there are about one hundred and thirty thousand savage Indians. Among the civilized people there are more of the mixed race than of the pure whites. The Indians who inhabited Paraguay when the Spaniards came were more civilized than most of the other tribes of the continent, and the Spaniards intermarried with them. Many of their sons and daughters also married Indians, and we find that nearly all the Paraguay people have Indian blood in their veins.

The Indians whom they married were the Guaranis (gwä-rä-nēs'), and to-day the Guarani language is more used by the common people than the Spanish. We shall take with us a guide who understands Guarani to act as interpreter during our tour, for we may be in places where the people cannot speak Spanish.

Paraguay has no large cities. The largest by far is Asuncion, which we are about to explore. It contains only thirty thousand people. Villa Rica (vēl'yä rē'ca), about one hundred miles to the east, is next in size. It has perhaps eight thousand. Other large towns are Villa Concepcion, two hundred and fifty miles north of Asuncion, on the Paraguay river, and Villa Encarnacion, in the south, on the north bank of the Parana river. Smaller towns and numerous villages are scattered about over the country.

The city of Asuncion is the business, social, and financial center, and has always been the principal town of Paraguay. As we go through it we shall find many modern improvements. It has banks, telegraphs, colleges, and newspapers. It has good houses, several large churches, and many buildings mossy with age.

Asuncion is one of the oldest cities of our hemisphere. Babies born in it had grown up and become gray-haired men and women before Captain John Smith started James-

Street in Asuncion.

town. It was long one of the chief centers of civilization of South America, and for some years was more important than either Buenos Aires or Montevideo.

In 1811 Paraguay declared itself independent. For many years afterwards it was governed by unscrupulous rulers who oppressed the people cruelly.

Finally, one of the rulers, named Lopez, finding it so easy to oppress his own people, thought he could dictate as he pleased to the nations about him. He offended Brazil, Uruguay, and Argentina, and they combined and declared war upon him. They marched with their armies against the Paraguayans, and although the latter fought bravely they could not withstand such a large force. The war lasted five years, and in the end nearly all the men and many of the women of Paraguay perished. The tyrant Lopez was killed.

Then Paraguay sued for peace. She lost much of her territory and became very poor. Asuncion had been almost destroyed, large parts of the country had been laid desolate, and of the people there were little more than women and children left.

Indeed, so many of the men were killed that to-day there are more women than men in the country. We notice this as we walk from the wharves up into Asuncion. It is early morning, and the streets are filled with women going to and from market. How like ghosts they look! Each is clad in white, with a long cotton sheet wrapped about her head, so that only her dark face shows. The most of them are barefooted, and they make no noise as they walk spiritlike through the streets.

There is one coming toward us who has a great jar upon her head and a load of firewood in her arms. She is walking rapidly, and her dark legs show out below her white skirts halfway to the knees. Behind her comes another white-sheeted figure, upon whose head is a great basket of oranges with a chunk of raw meat on top. The basket is perfectly balanced, and she walks along without touching her burden. There are other women carrying all sorts of things in the same way—bags of vegetables, pans of meat, bundles of firewood; in fact, they carry everything on their heads. It seems no trouble to keep the loads steady, for as we go by they do not lift up their hands, and take no pains to avoid being jostled.

We pass more women on our way to the market house, going through the chief business streets. The city is not large, and it takes but a short time to learn its most curious features. It is laid out in the Spanish style, the streets crossing one another at right angles, with a park or a plaza here and there. But few of the streets are paved. The others have a roadbed of deep sand as red as brick dust. This is the color of the best soil of Paraguay.

"There is one coming toward us."

The streets are wide, but the town is so up hill and down that there are but few carriages. The carts rattle as they go over the stones. Many of them are hauled by three mules abreast, which are driven at such a pace that we jump up on the sidewalk to get out of the way.

What curious houses! They are almost all of one story, built close to the sidewalk, in blocks, so that they form solid walls running from street to street. All have iron-barred windows, and the houses are painted each a different color. Here is one of sky blue, the next is rose pink, and over the way is one of pale yellow.

Here comes a policeman. He is dressed in a blue

uniform, with a long sword at his side. If he should arrest us he would take us into a red jail, and on the way we should pass the lilac-colored building in which Congress meets. We might see the cream-tinted palace from which the president rules, and should go by houses of every color.

Let us take a look at the business part of the town. The stores are not large, but they are stocked

"They carry everything on their heads."

with goods from all parts of the world. That building on the corner is the chief hotel of the country. It was once a palace of Lopez, the tyrant.

The market house is a block farther on. It looks more like a monastery than a market. It is a great one-story building, running about a hollow square, with a low roof which extends out upon all sides, over the cloisters or wide porches which run round it. It is painted Indian red, and the color forms a bright background for the strange figures about it. People are buying and selling at the meat stalls in the building. The court inside is filled with tables and benches, where all kinds of things Paraguayan are sold.

Let us stop in the porches and look about us. Every

part of the market is swarming with women. There are scores of women sitting on the bricks, with their wares spread out before them. Others stand behind the butcher counters, and with knives and saws cut up great chunks of meat for their customers. Others have vegetables, laces, and jewelry, which they beseech you to buy.

What a chatter they make as they bargain! There are no scales and no measures. See this vegetable woman

"The lilac-colored building in which Congress meets."

who is squatting almost under our feet. She has a stock of green peas which she has arranged in piles on the bricks. There is about a pint in each pile, and the customer buys by eye measure. Each purchaser brings a cloth with her to wrap up what she buys, for the market women furnish neither paper nor string.

In going through the market we can learn much concerning the chief products of Paraguay. We see tobacco sold everywhere, and we shall find that Paraguay raises much tobacco for export. The greater part of the tobacco, however, is consumed at home. Three fourths of the women we meet have cigars in their mouths. Both buyers and sellers are smoking like chimneys. Some of the mar-

Market, Asuncion.

ket women are chewing cigars, and others are rolling up leaf tobacco to smoke. We see small girls smoking and chewing, and boys of six and eight years smoke without stint.

Among other things sold in large quantities are manioc and oranges. Manioc is a root which in Paraguay takes the place of both potatoes and wheat as food. Its roots grow in great bunches, each root about the size of a carrot. There are two varieties. One of these is boiled or roasted much like a potato; the other must first be ground and squeezed to take out a poisonous juice which it has in it. After this it becomes a flour, and is eaten in soup, in stews, and in other ways.

XXIX. PARAGUAY—A TRIP INTO THE INTERIOR.

TO-DAY we are traveling through the interior of Paraguay. We have taken our seats in one of the first-class cars of the railroad, which runs one hundred miles east from Asuncion to Villa Rica, and thence goes southward toward the Parana river. The engineer has thrown a lot of wood into the furnace, but the cars go so slowly that we are able to see much of the country as we pass through.

Leaving Asuncion, we go by the villas of rich Paraguayans, pass the agricultural college, where the boys are playing under the palm trees, and then on into great pastures bordered with bushy woods and spotted here and there with small clumps of trees.

The lands are as rich as our prairies, and resemble them, save that thickets and groves everywhere give shade for the cattle. We are in a vast sea of grass, which seems to be flowing in and out among islands of woods. In the summer the woods are fragrant and the plains are covered with most beautiful flowers. Paraguay has miles of such pastures, and upon them two million cattle are feeding.

There is a big herd now on our left. There are men on horseback moving to and fro among the beasts and driving them this way and that. They are probably picking out the fat beeves for shipment, or they may be about to brand the stock.

A little farther off to the right we see a village. We pass villages at every few miles, and there are many small towns at which the train stops. The most of the people of

Paraguay live in villages. Their houses are merely thatched huts with walls made of woven poles covered with mud.

We can easily visit one while the train waits at a station. What a rude hut it is! It is composed of two parts, a room about fifteen feet square and a shed. The shed has no walls. It is merely an extension of the thatched roof which covers the closed room, and is upheld by poles.

The people live in the shed during the day. There are hammocks hung to the poles, and men and women are

"What a rude hut it is!"

sitting in them. Naked babies and half-naked children play about on the dirt floor. The climate is warm in the summer, and it is the breeze which sweeps through the shed that makes life endurable.

There is but little furniture. We see only a table and one or two chairs. The chief object of interest is a log stood upon end. It is about as high as your waist; there is a hole dug out of its top. Before the log a woman is standing. She has a heavy stick or club in her hand, which she is lifting up and dropping on some corn which she has put in the hole. Such logs are the grist mills of Paraguay. In them the women pound their corn and manioc to flour.

We find the people hospitable. They live simply, but do not seem to care for anything except something to eat, a little liquor to drink, and enough cigars to smoke all the day through.

Indian Children.

Now we are again on the train, moving out through the fields. What are those odd little hills which stand out like small haycocks among the green grass? There are hundreds of them, dark-red mounds, spotting the fields and looking as though they had been thrown up by man. Now we are passing some mounds as high as our waists, and now we have come to a field in which there are thousands which hardly reach to our knees. What can they be? They look like nothing but dirt. They are dirt. They are the mounds of ant cities.

Paraguay has hundreds of millions of ants, which throw

up such mounds all over the country. In some places there are so many that they destroy the pastures, and when the people wish to cultivate the ground they first must fight the ants. Every hill must be dug up, for there are as many ants below as above ground. After being dug up the hills are set on fire. They burn easily, and in this way the ants are destroyed.

The ants sometimes burrow into the houses, and a woman may awake in the morning to find a great mound of dirt on her parlor floor, the ants having decided to build a village there. She sweeps out the dirt and deluges the brick floor with hot water, sometimes to find, a morning or so later, that the ants are again besieging her dwelling.

We pass many trees on our way through the country. Even on the plains there are woods always in sight. Paraguay has large forests containing excellent lumber. Some of its trees could be used for shipbuilding, for the wood can remain under the water for years and still not decay. Other trees have a fine grain, so that they would make beautiful furniture, and others are good for tan bark, dyewoods, and many sorts of things.

As we think of this, it seems strange that these great forests do not supply all South America with lumber. It would surely be cheaper to get wood for Argentina, Chile, and Peru from here than from our forests in Oregon and New England. Yes, it seems so at first, but not after you have studied the matter.

The Paraguay woods are so heavy that they will not float. The trees must be loaded upon carts and dragged through the forests, or they must be put upon railroad cars and brought to Asuncion before they can be shipped down the Paraguay to Buenos Aires. In our country we have the snow to help us get the trees to the rivers, and our lumber floats. Here it costs a great deal to get the logs out of the forests, and the freight rates on the river steamers are so high that it is much cheaper for the people along the coasts of South America to bring their lumber from North America, more than five thousand miles away, than to buy it here, nearer home.

"As delicate as cobwebs."

But we are nearing a station. Get out your money for that crowd of women peddlers who are coming to canvass the cars. Here they are now. One has a pile of straw hats fitted one into the other on the top of her head. She will sell one for fifteen cents of our money. There is a bareheaded girl with a platter of cakes each as large around as a one-gallon crock, and there are others with fruits and baby clothes and fine laces. Notice the lace handkerchiefs which that dark-faced little girl spreads out before you. They are as delicate as cobwebs, and are made of fibers grown in the country. Lace-making is one of the great industries of Paraguayan women, and you can buy beautiful things very cheap.

Let us get out on the platform and follow the crowd rushing toward the women squatted down on the bricks. They are peddlers, but their wares are too heavy to be brought into the train. Some are selling meat. Yes, selling beefsteaks at a station! They have baskets of raw beef before them, and are peddling it out to the passengers.

TRIP INTO THE INTERIOR.

What a lot of the women are smoking! Nearly every one has a cigar in her mouth. If it were not for this we might think some of the girls very pretty. They have cream-colored faces, dark eyes, soft black hair, and fairly good teeth. Nearly all are in their bare feet, and as we walk we have to be careful not to step on their toes with our heavy shoes.

But here is a maiden with a lot of oranges piled up before her. Let us see how many we can get for a medio,

"You often see a hundred women trotting along thus in single file."

which is about three quarters of a cent of our money. I point to the oranges and say in my poor Spanish: "Quantos por un medio, señorita?"

"Ocho," replies the girl, as she puffs a volume of smoke out of her nostrils and hands me eight golden balls.

We find the oranges as sweet as the best of our Florida fruit. They have a fine flavor, and are so cheap that we buy more and more as we go from station to station.

Paraguay is beyond all others the country of oranges. You see orange trees in every thicket, and out of every forest they peep at you with their thousand golden eyes. The mud huts of the farmers stand amid orange groves, and in some places there are so many oranges that they rot on the ground.

Oranges are exported by millions down the Paraguay river to Uruguay and Argentina. They are brought to the banks of the river from the orchards in ox carts so large that each will hold about five thousand oranges. The fruit is dumped out like so many potatoes, the drivers taking no more care in emptying their carts than our drivers do when they dump dirt in repairing the roads.

Loading a Steamer.

At the towns along the Paraguay river during the season there are great piles of oranges, with scores of women kneeling before them, picking up the fruit and putting it into baskets. As soon as a basket is full it is handed to a woman carrier, who raises it to her head, and thus balancing it trots along with it over a broad walk above the water to the steamer. You often see a hundred women trotting along thus in single file. Each has on the top of her head a round basket filled with oranges. She does not touch her hand to the basket, and walks rapidly over the springing boards.

At the steamer the hold is first filled with oranges. Then a wire netting is stretched about the deck, making a fence as high as a man's head, within which the golden fruit is piled.

XXX. PARAGUAY—A CURIOUS TEA— THE CHACO AND ITS INDIANS.

WE have returned from our trip in the interior and are again on our way to the north. There are boats twice a week from Asuncion to Villa Concepcion, and once a fortnight a Brazilian steamer calls at the Paraguay ports on its way into the wilds of southern Brazil. We resolve to go first to Villa Concepcion, and from there to make some tours through the forests on both sides of the river.

Shortly after leaving Asuncion the Paraguay narrows. The scenes along it are of great beauty. The banks are well wooded. We now and then see a clearing in which there is a village with orange trees hanging above the thatched huts. There are more wild birds than there were farther south. Alligators are numerous, and when we rise before day we now and then catch a glimpse of a panther swimming across the river, as they sometimes do about dawn. We pass the mouth of the river Confuso, and come to land again at Villa Concepcion.

Here we see scores of men bringing bales of mate, or Paraguay tea, down to the wharves and putting them on the steamer. Mate is one of the chief exports of Paraguay. It commands a high price in all South American countries below the equator, and, indeed, Paraguay produces so much of it every year that if the product were all cooked up at once it would make a cup of tea for every man, woman, and child in the world.

Mate was used as tea before Columbus discovered America. The Indians induced the Spaniards to try it, and it has now become the favorite beverage of many South American nations. Argentina uses seven times as much mate as coffee, and twenty-six times as much mate as Chinese or Japanese tea. Brazil, which raises more coffee than any other country in the world, uses a great deal of mate, and the people of Uruguay and Chile prefer it to all other drinks.

But what is this tea that so tickles the South American palate? It is easy to learn. There is a woman on the steamer who is drinking some now. Our cabin boy will bring us a bowl if we ask him. It is served in a round gourd as big as a baseball. The gourd has a handle fitted into the side, and you drink your tea boiling hot. A spoonful of the powdered leaves is put into the bowl, the hot water is poured in, and the tea is ready for use. You do not put the bowl to your mouth, but suck the mate up through a tube. The tube is called a bombilla (bombēl′ya). Sometimes it is of silver, sometimes of brass, and among the poorer people often a hollow reed. The metal tube ends in a bulb. This bulb is pierced with holes, so that the tea is strained as you suck it into your mouth.

Here comes the boy with our mate. Be careful how you put the bombilla between your lips. The boiling tea has made it so hot that it may take off the skin. Wet your lips first and then try it. How bitter the tea is! It does not taste at all good at first drinking, but you will come to like it, and will probably want it again and again during our tour.

The tea is quite stimulating. It is said to be good for the brain, and it will refresh you when you are tired. Many South Americans take nothing else for their early breakfast. If the gauchos of the Argentina pampas can have their mate in the morning they will gallop on horseback all day, and be satisfied if they get their first meal when we are eating our suppers.

Gathering Mate.

We leave the ship at Villa Concepcion and go many miles inland to see the tea forests. They are called yerbales. The plants which furnish the mate are low bushes which grow among the other trees. They are much like the holly bush, and sometimes grow as high as a small orange tree. The leaves are green all the year round, and it is the younger leaves which make the best tea.

The people who gather the mate leaves are called yerbateros (yer-bä-tā'rōs). They chop off the small branches and bring them in bundles to the camps which have been put up in the forest. Here there are drying houses, each consisting of a framework with an arched roof of poles woven together and upheld by posts. Under the roof there is a floor of clay, so well hammered down that it is as hard as stone.

The branches are taken from the men as soon as they are brought in by other laborers, who weave them in and out among the poles of the roof, so that the framework is thatched with the leaves. Then a slow fire is built on the clay floor, and the leaves are thus roasted until they are perfectly dry. Sweet-smelling woods are used for fuel, and the fires are kept up from daylight until dark, great care being taken that there be but little smoke.

When the leaves have become perfectly dry the fire is removed and the leaves are pushed through the framework, crumbling up as they fall to the floor. They are now pounded with flat wooden clubs until they become a coarse powder. This forms the mate of commerce.

The mate powder is now ready for packing. This is done in bags of rawhide. The skin of a large ox is taken just as it comes fresh from the animal, and sewed up, forming a bag like a square pillowcase about three feet in length. Into this the mate is put, being so pounded down that when the bag is full it forms a solid bale. Now the top is sewed up with thongs of green hide, and the bale is placed in the sun. The skin dries as the sun's rays strike it, shrinking in and pressing the mate tighter and tighter, until the whole seems one solid rock.

About a million dollars' worth of such bales of tea are made in Paraguay each year, and we shall see mule trains loaded with them making their way toward Villa Concepcion and the other ports of the country.

We meet many Indians as we go through the forests. Some of the more civilized are employed gathering mate; others are savage, and we must be careful how we go about by ourselves. We find this especially so in the Chaco, in which we make some journeys after coming back to Villa Concepcion. The Paraguayan Chaco is inhabited almost entirely by Indians, some of whom are of the strangest tribes of our hemisphere.

Toba Indian.

There are some Indians who go naked all the year round. The Tobas, for instance, wear but little clothes, except when they come into the presence of white people or cross the Paraguay river to trade. These Indians are very tall, some being six feet in height. Their skin is so thick that it is said they can walk on thorny ground without sandals. The men are good hunters and fishers, but the women do most of the work, planting the crops, cooking the meals, and weaving the blankets. The Toba women tatoo themselves in blue and red lines, and dye their hair yellow.

Another tribe is the Lenguas. They are experts in taming wild animals and birds. Farther north there are Indians who were noted as oarsmen when the Spanish first came. They were terrible warriors, and when on the rivers they had oars tipped with spearheads, so that in close combats they could use them as weapons.

Many of the South American Indians do not live in wigwams. Some wander from place to place, having no houses whatever. Others have villages with huts so built together that one roof of straw thatch covers several

Indian Family.

houses. One part of the hut is used for cooking and another for sleeping. The people sleep upon skins when they have them, otherwise on the bare ground. The women are good cooks, and some are quite cleanly, washing their pots and pans at the close of each meal. They have but few cooking utensils. They use shells for spoons. Every one carries his own knife, but forks are unknown.

Their chief weapons are bows and arrows, some of the Indians being so skillful that they can bring down the most savage beasts of the forest.

The Chaco is a great hunting country. We can shoot alligators along any of the small streams, and in traveling

"There are jaguars in the Chaco."

near the water at night we have to step carefully, lest we get our feet into their mouths. There are jaguars in the Chaco so strong that one of them can easily carry off an ox or a horse. They do not attack men unless they are very hungry, and if we meet them in the underbrush a yell will usually drive them away.

As we camp overnight in the forest, however, we are now and then aroused by the crack of a branch, and, looking up, see the fierce eyes of a brute flashing out of the darkness. We find we have to send away our dogs. The jaguars hate dogs, and we are told that for this reason it is dangerous to travel with them through the forest.

Among the most dangerous animals of the Chaco are the wild dogs. There is one called the aguara guazu, which is a beast of prey. It is not quite three feet long, and is for all the world like a sharp-eared yellow dog with black legs. It has a sharp muzzle, and its ears are always erect. It has a bushy tail like that of a fox. It has a hoarse bark, which can be heard a long way off. This dog lives in the swamps and goes hunting at night. It attacks sheep and cattle, and will fight for its life with a jaguar.

Peccary.

But what is that shrill, whistling cry which we hear night after night as we go through the forests? That is a tapir, an animal with a head much like a pig, although it is as big as a pony. It is very dangerous if interfered with, and its skin is so thick that it is almost impossible to kill it unless you hit it just in the forehead or behind the shoulder.

Even more dangerous, however, are the peccaries, which are found in great numbers in parts of the Chaco. They are little wild pigs with sharp teeth, which go in herds of eight or ten, and sometimes in droves of fifty or more.

They are very ferocious, and often attack travelers who come near them on foot. If we should meet them, our best way would be to climb a tree and shoot at them from

Tapir.

there. Peccaries live on roots and fallen fruits. They eat the wild oranges and the nuts of the woods, and often come at night close to the Paraguayan villages to get the oranges which grow in the gardens.

There are many other curious beasts which live in these forests. We might stay for weeks and have excellent hunting, for in addition to the dangerous animals there are many species of deer, antelope, and different kinds of birds. The mail steamer, however, is almost due at Villa Concepcion, and we must hurry back if we would go in it to Brazil.

Brazil.

XXXI. IN BRAZIL—THE WILDS OF MATTO GROSSO.

TO-DAY we are again on the Paraguay river. We have been traveling for some time upon it, and are now in the wilds of southern Brazil. Our ship is winding in and out among mountains, at the bases of which are fern trees and tall palms. Now we go by forests which are so filled with vines and creepers that we can see only a few feet back from the banks, and we could not possibly make our way into the interior without an ax or a knife.

What is that furry face with the twinkling black eyes which grins at us out of the branches, chattering now and then, and gnashing its teeth? That is a monkey. There are thousands of them in these forests. That great red-and-blue bird with a hooked bill as long as your finger, which you see farther on, is a toucan. There are all sorts of strange birds in the trees.

There are many wild animals. See that white deer there in the bushes. Those black things near the shore, which look like small logs, are alligators. They have been disturbed by the waves of the steamer and are scrambling upon the banks. Some are diving down into the water, and others are swimming to get out of the way of our boat.

Look at the Indians on the other side of the river. They are half naked, and they shake their spears at us as we steam on our way. This part of Brazil is full of wild Indians; there are more Indians than whites. There are vast regions farther on to the west which have no people but savages.

As we proceed, the wildness increases, save here and there where we pass farmhouses cut out of the woods.

Now our boat stops at one for fresh meat. The cattle are lifted on board by their horns. We are supplied with fish from the river and the small streams flowing into it. There are so many fish here that you have only to explode a dynamite cartridge under the water, and dozens of fish, killed by the shock, will float on their backs on all sides of your boat.

At the boundary of Brazil we pass a fortification with soldiers about it. This is Fort Coimbra; a little farther on we pass the Brazilian arsenal of Godario, and soon after this reach the little city of Corumba'. This port has the only customs house of this part of Brazil. Inspectors in blue uniforms board our steamer as it stops at the wharves, and our baggage must be spread out before them.

"There are thousands of them in these forests."

While the steamer waits, we visit the city, which is on

a high bluff overlooking the river. It has about ten thousand people, and it looks so much like Asuncion that we might think we were back among the Paraguayans, were it not that the language is strange. The people of

A Farmhouse.

Corumba all speak Portuguese. This is the language of Brazil, and from now on for weeks we shall hear little else. It sounds much like Spanish, but is a little harsher and not so melodious.

We are now traveling in the state of Matto Grosso. The words mean " Great Forest," and the state of Matto Grosso is one of the wildest parts of Brazil. It has vast territories covered with woods which have never been trodden by white men, and there are plains in it upon which thousands of wild cattle are feeding. It is a large state, being twice as large as Texas and more than ten times as large as New York. The part through which we are traveling contains the only white settlements, and Cuyaba (coo-ya-bä'), the city where we next stop, is its capital, the metropolis of interior Brazil.

The way we came up the Paraguay river is the only easy route to Matto Grosso. There are no railroads in this part of Brazil, and although Cuyaba is not more than

"At the boundary of Brazil we pass a fortification with soldiers about it."

nine hundred miles from Rio de Janeiro, its officials and mails have to go more than thirty-eight hundred miles to reach it. They come on steamers down the Atlantic to Montevideo, and then steam on through the Rio de la Plata, Parana, and Paraguay to Corumba. Here smaller ships are taken, and they travel up other rivers until they land at last at this point, which is farther by this way from the ocean than Salt Lake City is distant from Washington. It takes more than a month for a letter now to come from

Cuyaba.

Rio de Janeiro to Cuyaba, but at some time a railroad will be built overland, upon which the trip can be made in less than two days.

At present almost all traveling is done upon the water. We do not find horses and mules common here, and away from the river we are offered bullocks for riding animals. We see women and men riding bullocks, the women sitting astride like the men. Bullocks are used for plowing. They drag huge carts over the road, and they serve as pack animals. It seems very funny when we first climb on their backs, but we find some of them good saddle beasts, their gait being a sort of pace.

We are surprised at the size of Cuyaba. It has about twenty thousand people, and, for such an out-of-the-way place, many modern improvements. It has street cars, waterworks, and a cathedral. It has colleges and schools. There is music on Sunday afternoon in the plaza, and we go there often at eventide to enjoy ourselves under the great palm trees, whose fanlike leaves move to and fro in the breeze.

An Indian of Matto Grosso.

The region about Cuyaba is a rich farming country, and we are told that there is gold in the hills near the city. There are mines close to the town, which are still being worked, and after a big rain the Cuyaba boys go out and search for grains of gold in the streets which have been flooded by the streams from the hills. We are told that the boys are often well paid for their trouble, and we get down on our knees to see if perhaps we can find a stray golden nugget, but, alas! there is nothing but sand.

We spend some time in the woods near Cuyaba. They are full of strange plants, one of which is exported to all parts of the world. This is ipecac, a small shrub which grows in clumps or patches in the moist parts of the forests. It is often used to make children vomit when they have swallowed a penny or eaten some indigestible or poisonous thing.

We see Indians hunting for it as we go through the forest. When they find one of the plants they pry it out of the ground with a stick, raising it very carefully to save all the roots, for the roots form the article of commerce.

"We are offered bullocks for riding animals."

After they are taken out they are dried for three days in the sun. They are then broken up, cleaned, and packed in bags of cow's skin, and thus shipped to the factories of Europe.

XXXII. SOUTHERN BRAZIL.

WE have been traveling more than a month since we left Matto Grosso. From Cuyaba we sailed back into the Paraguay river, and on down through the Parana to Montevideo. There we took a coasting steamer, and we are now making our way from port to port along the shores of southern Brazil.

What an immense country Brazil is! It is hard for us to realize its extent. The states which look so small on the map widen out as we travel over them, and we are struck with the fact that we are in one of the large countries of the world. There are only four other nations which own so much land as the Brazilians. Their republic is larger than the whole United States, without Alaska and our outlying islands. It is longer from north to south than the distance from Pittsburg to San Francisco, and its width from east to west is greater than the distance from New York to Salt Lake City. It contains more than 3,228,000 square miles, almost half of all the land of South America.

Brazil has more than half the people of South America. Its population is estimated at eighteen millions. Its people are different in their origin as well as in their customs from the other South Americans. Brazil was discovered and settled by the Portuguese, and its people speak the Portuguese tongue. We often hear South America called the Spanish-American continent. It would be quite as proper to call it the Portuguese-American continent, on account of the size and population of Brazil.

Such a vast territory must have many kinds of soil and many climates. Brazil extends from north of the equator far to the southward, and the weather of the different regions changes also according to their different elevations above the sea. In the low Amazon valley it is almost always hot, but the winds from the ocean sweep up the wide river and make some parts of it healthful. South of the Amazon valley, a little back from the coast, the land is high, so that it has quite as salubrious a climate as many parts of our country. Some of the plateaus, from lack of rain, are deserts, others upon which heavy rains fall are covered with woods, and upon others much farther south can be grown all the crops of our Southern States.

Near the borders of Uruguay there are pastures as good as those of Argentina. There the thermometer never rises above 100° in the summer month of January, and there in midwinter (July) there is often snow on the ground.

"There are vast pastures."

We reach this region first as we sail along the coast. We stop at Porto Alegre (pōr'tō ä-lä'grä), the capital of the state of Rio Grande do Sul. This state is devoted to raising wheat and meat. Its pastures are much like those of Argentina; it has beef factories such as we saw on the Uruguay river, in which hundreds of oxen are killed every day for jerked or dried beef.

Porto Alegre has thirty-five thousand people. It has daily newspapers, colleges, public schools, and fine stores. We are surprised to see that the faces of more than half of the people are German. We speak German to the clerks in the stores, and meet many little German children on the streets. Rio Grande do Sul is largely settled by Germans. They have come here from Europe, and find the climate quite as good as that of their fatherland on the other side of the Atlantic. Many of them own large farms, stores, and factories.

Leaving Porto Alegre, we go north to Santos (sän'tōs), sail up a wide bay, and come into a harbor which is filled with ships from Europe and the United States, loading and unloading freight. Santos is the chief port for a large part of southern Brazil. It is where the most of the coffee is shipped, and it is visited regularly by twenty lines of ocean steamers, which come here to bring goods and to carry away coffee to other parts of the world. We see some ships loading coffee; others are taking off bags of rice from India, boxes of codfish from Massachusetts and Newfoundland, coal and cottons from England, and lumber from the pine lands of Maine.

It is a busy scene, and we are anxious to get to the shore. Now we have hired a dark-faced Portuguese boatman, and have made our way among the ships to the wharves. What a strong smell of coffee surrounds us! The air is full of it. It comes from the warehouses back of the wharves, in which we see half-naked negroes shoveling coffee from piles into bags. It comes from the bags which other negroes are carrying on to the steamers, and also from those big wagons loaded with coffee on their way through the city. Here the coffee bags are being lifted by steam cranes from the wharves to the steamers; there men are trotting along with bags on their backs, and over there they are carrying the bags on their heads and emptying them out on the floors of the factories, where the coffee is to be cleaned and rebagged before it is ready for shipment. We shall see more of this in Rio de Janeiro later on.

Santos has about twenty-five thousand people. It is a town of two- and three-story houses built along narrow streets on the edge of the harbor. It is very unhealthful.

Loading Coffee.

It frequently has yellow fever, and strangers are liable to get the disease. We are warned not to stay long, and hurry on to the station and take tickets for the more salubrious city of São Paulo (souN pou'lō), which lies on the plateau over the mountains, about forty-seven miles back from the sea.

The ride is delightful. Leaving the city, we are carried through fields of bananas, the tall plants bending down with great bunches of yellow fruit. We go through a jungle of tropical vegetation, and then ascend the mountains, winding this way and that through a dense forest in which there are millions of orchids. The trees are loaded with these beautiful air plants. They are bound together with creepers and vines, and the whole forms a forest wall on each side of the track, so dense that we can see only a few feet through the trees.

"A great feat of civil engineering."

The railroad which takes us up the coast range is a great feat of civil engineering. The ordinary locomotives are uncoupled from the cars at the foot of the mountains, and our train is divided into sections of two cars each. Around each two cars a steel rope, or cable, is wrapped, and this cable is fastened to a third car which has a brake, so that the engineers can keep it from sliding back if an accident should happen on the way up. Another cable is joined to the grip car. This cable extends several miles up the mountains to a stationary steam engine. When the men on the car give a signal, the engineer above moves a lever, and a great wheel begins to revolve, rolling up the cable, and so pulling our cars on their way to the station. When we reach the first engine house, another cable is attached, connecting us with an engine house still higher up, and so the cars are dragged on until at the third station they have been taken about a half-mile higher up in the air than they were when they started. At this point the cars are again fastened together, and a railroad locomotive rapidly carries our train over a gently sloping plateau, and lands us in São Paulo.

Here we remain several days. São Paulo is the largest city of southern Brazil. It has about two hundred thousand people, and it is one of the most enterprising cities of the republic.

It is more like one of our own towns than any South American place we have yet seen. It is the capital of the state of São Paulo, which has some of the best of the coffee lands. The city has government buildings as good as those of the State capitals of our country, and some of its schoolhouses are as fine as any schoolhouse in the United States.

We stay overnight at the hotel, and upon rising take a walk through the town. It is early morning, and the children are going to school. There are scores of bright-faced little girls without hats, in black dresses. There are little boys wearing caps, coats, and knee breeches, but with their legs bare almost to their shoes, where their short stockings end. Each child has a bag of books in his hand; they are trudging along over the cobblestone streets.

In São Paulo.

Get out of the way of the street cars! They come in a train, one car following another until a dozen have passed. When they are beyond the business part of the city they will branch out in various directions.

What odd cars they are! Some of them are loaded with freight. These are second-class cars, intended for people going to and from market. They are used chiefly by the servants, for a man with a basket or bundle is not allowed to ride in a regular passenger car.

What is that queer vehicle coming this way? I mean that two-wheeled carriage drawn by the pony, with the seat high up off the ground. That is a tilbury, a favorite vehicle in all Brazilian cities, and well fitted for a hilly town like São Paulo.

What a lot of negroes we meet everywhere! They make us feel as though we were at home in our southern States. Brazil has more negroes in proportion to the whites than any part of our country. It had slaves much longer than we had, but now all have been freed, and people of African blood have equal rights with all others.

Here come three Africans now. Listen to that laugh. It sounds like the jolly yah! yah! yah! of our dark-skinned Americans. Let us wait here on the corner and hear some of their jokes as they pass.

Why don't we laugh? That man on the left said something funny, and his fellows and himself are convulsed. They are speaking quite loud, and though we hear what they say we cannot see the joke. They are speaking in Portuguese, the language used by both colored and whites in Brazil.

XXXIII. IN THE LAND OF COFFEE.

BRAZIL is the chief coffee country in the world. It produces more than two thirds of all the coffee used by man. This very morning there are millions of people in the United States who have had a cup of Brazilian coffee with their breakfasts. Most of the coffee we drink comes from Brazil.

Coffee grows best in a semitropical climate. The plants must not have frost, but at the same time they must not be spoiled by the heat. The climate of many parts of Brazil is just right for them. Indeed, it is said that coffee can be grown in every one of the Brazilian states. The best coffee regions, however, are to be found on the highlands west and south of Rio de Janeiro. Here the land is from one thousand to three thousand feet above the sea. It is gently rolling, and it has thousands of hillsides which are covered with coffee plantations.

The best of all coffee lands, indeed, lie in the state of São Paulo, where we now are. They are several hundred miles back from the coast, and by taking the train we can visit some of the richest coffee estates of the world.

The largest plantations are so far from the city of São Paulo that it would take us almost a day to reach them by railroad. We ride through rolling plains covered with grass; now we pass clumps of palms whose tops extend out like great fans, and then go on through forests of hardwood trees, the trunks of which are twisted about like

Banana Plantation.

THE LAND OF COFFEE. 259

corkscrews. The trees are bound together in a mat made by the long vines and creepers which hang down from their branches. Now we pass a banana plantation, and now we see lemon and orange trees in the gardens by the side of the road.

It is dry, for this part of Brazil has not had rain for some weeks. There is a cool wind blowing, but the air which comes over the plowed fields is loaded with dust.

Coffee Plantation.

The boys who peddle fruit at the stations are covered with dust, and we find ourselves sneezing as the stuff gets into our noses.

What queer dust it is! It is as red as brick dust, and everything it touches turns red. We are soon as red as

Sioux Indians; our collars have red streaks at the neck, and our coats look as though they were dusted with Cayenne pepper. There is red on the fences and trees and on the green bushes. We see wide streaks of red cutting their way through the reddish-green grass. Those streaks are the roads, for the very ground itself under the sod is the color of pounded-up brick.

This red land is the famous coffee soil of Brazil. Its color comes from the large amount of iron mixed with the other matter composing it, and the redder the soil the better it is thought to be for the raising of coffee.

About fifty miles from São Paulo the plantations begin, and from there on we ride all day long among hills covered with coffee bushes.

Most of the coffee is grown upon large plantations. The estate we visit has about five million trees. It is indeed the largest coffee plantation of the world. It is so large that we could not walk around the outside of it in one day, if we began when the sun rose and kept walking steadily until dark. It is so large that its managers have railroad tracks extending from the factories to all parts of it, and we are carried from one coffee field to another on a little steam engine which is kept for hauling the crops.

The ride is a beautiful one. We spend hours going through one coffee field after another. There is nothing but coffee bushes about us as far as our eyes can reach. The whole land is covered with a mantle of green, striped here and there with bands of bright red. The green mantle is the coffee bushes, and the red stripes the roads. The bushes are laid out in regular lines, and they extend on and on until they lose themselves in the sky at the tops of the hills in the distance.

As we proceed we can see the coffee plants in their

different stages of growth. In some fields they are not so high as our knees, and in others they are three times as high as our heads. Here men are plowing the fields, driving carefully through the green trees, turning up the red soil. There boys are down on their knees pulling out the weeds, and farther on a gang of laborers is laying out new rows among the stumps of the freshly cleared land, and putting in coffee plants from the nurseries.

We shall learn, as we go, what a great deal of work is required to produce even one cup of coffee. Upon this plantation five thousand people are busy raising the crop and preparing it for the market. In the first place, let me tell you just what the coffee beans are. As you see them in the stores they are far different from the coffee berries which are picked from the trees. The beans are the seeds of the berries. You can see some of the berries on that bush over there. They are just like dark-red cherries. They hang in clusters close to the limbs, among the green leaves. In each berry are one or two seeds, which form the coffee of commerce. How they are got out we shall see at the factory later on.

Coffee Tree.

Here in the fields we must learn how the bushes are grown.

The beans must first be sown in seed beds. They soon sprout, and little green plants shoot up through the soil. After a few months they have grown a foot high. They are now ready for transplanting to the fields, where they are to become big coffee bushes, or, as they are sometimes called, coffee trees.

Picking Coffee Berries.

The plants are set quite deep in the ground. A little basin is dug out for each one, and at first sticks or leaves are spread over it to protect it from the hot rays of the sun. It is carefully hoed to keep down the weeds, and when it is four years old it begins to bear fruit.

A good tree should produce three or four pounds of coffee beans a year, and in the rich coffee lands of South Brazil a tree often bears crops for thirty years, and sometimes more.

The coffee bushes begin to blossom in December, and in April or May the berries are ripe and the picking begins. There are then hundreds of men, women, and children moving among the bushes. They are picking the ripe red berries into baskets and carrying them to the cars which are to take them to the factories on the plantation.

Carting Coffee.

During our journey we see here and there long rows of one-story houses, and near them large buildings which look like machine shops. The small houses are the homes of the laborers on the estate. The big ones are the places in which the coffee seeds are taken out of the berries and prepared for the markets. They contain machinery of different kinds for extracting the seeds, and near them are the drying floors, great fields paved with cement, upon which the coffee beans are dried in the sun after they are taken out of the berries.

But first let us see how the seeds are extracted. There are some berries which have just come in from the fields. Take one up and look at it. It is just like a cherry, and almost as soft. Bite into it if you will. It is not bad to taste, though it is not much like coffee. Just inside the skin is a pulp, and within this are two half-round coffee beans with their flat sides touching each other. Take out the seeds. They do not look green like the coffee of commerce. They are white. Bite one of them again and

Drying Coffee.

you find that it has two skins. The outer skin is white. It is like parchment. The inner skin is as thin as the finest tissue paper you can imagine. The outside skin is called the parchment skin, and that within the silver skin, for it is much like silver spun out as fine as a cobweb. Both of these must be taken off before the coffee can be sent to our markets.

The first thing to be done is to get off the pulp. For this purpose the berries are thrown into a hopper and run through machines which squash the pulp without hurting the seeds. By these machines the berries are reduced to a mush of pulp and seeds. The mush is now carried over a long copper cylinder about two feet in diameter. In the cylinder there are hundreds of holes, each big enough for a coffee bean to pass through it. As the mush falls upon

"Most of them are Italians."

the cylinder, the beans go through the holes and are carried into a little canal, from which they float off into great vats.

They are next scoured clean in a tank in which a great screw moves round and round among the beans, leaving them at the end as white as snow.

The next process is drying. The white beans are spread out upon the drying platforms, and are left in the sun for several weeks until every one of them has become as dry as a bone. They are carefully watched at this time. Men stir them about with wooden rakes, so that they may be evenly dried, and cover them up at night and when it rains, so that they may not get wet.

This requires great care and much work, but when the beans are thoroughly dried they are by no means ready for sale. Each little bean has to be skinned. It has to be undressed, as it were. Its parchment coat must be taken off, and its silver-skin underclothes removed, so that it may be sent out in its olive-green nakedness to our markets.

To do this it is thrown into machines which break the skins. It is next carried into fanning mills, in which the skins are blown out in one place in the shape of chaff, like the chaff of a thrashing machine, and the coffee seeds, now olive green, flow out by themselves.

The seeds are of different sizes, some large and some small, some round and some almost flat. They must be separated and graded before they are ready for shipment. This is done by passing them over a series of sieves in which there are holes of different sizes, so that the grains of each kind are gathered together, and they flow out through different pipes into bags, ready to be shipped to the markets of the world.

The coffee bags are of one size. Each will hold one hundred and thirty-two pounds. As soon as a bag is full it is sewed up at the top and dragged off to the side. Later on it is taken on the cars to Rio de Janeiro or Santos, and there loaded upon ships which carry it to the United States or to Europe.

We spend some time in going about among the laborers on the estate. Most of them are Italians, who have taken the place of the negro slaves who were the coffee workers of Brazil a few years ago.

We see that the plantation is carefully managed. It has its overseers, its bookkeepers and accountants, who try to see that not a cent goes to waste. There is a large store upon it, at which the laborers can buy food, and it has its own bakery, foundry, and sawmills. It is indeed a little world of its own, which has grown up here in the heart of South America to produce the coffee which we drink at our meals.

XXXIV. RIO DE JANEIRO.

WE are again on shipboard this morning. We have gone back to Santos and taken the steamer for Rio, and are now sailing into its wonderful harbor. We might have traveled from São Paulo to Rio de Janeiro by rail, but we wish to pass through the harbor of Rio, for it is the most beautiful harbor of the whole world. It has been compared with the harbor of the Golden Horn of Constantinople; but the author has seen both places, and he thinks the Bay of Rio de Janeiro far finer. This bay is much the shape of a great pear, and is so large that all the ships of the world could be anchored in it at one time.

About the harbor, just a little back from its shores, rise the Organ Mountains, covered with the rich green of the tropics. Some of the hills are of curious shapes. One looks like a hunchback, and the people have called it the "Corcovado," a Portuguese word which means hunchback. Its top is more than a half-mile above the city, and there is a little railroad which goes up it. Another hill summit is much like the round head of a negro, the trees upon it at a distance looking like the wool on the head of an African. Others remind us of battlements and forts, and all together they form a great wall of green about the harbor.

We enter the bay at the smaller end, or the stem of the pear. We go in between two forts, passing through a narrow channel. On one side of us is a great mountain of rock formed like a sugar loaf. It rises almost straight up

"We go in between two forts."

from the sea to a height greater than that of two Washington monuments one on top of the other. On the opposite side are islands so close that at a distance we fear we may graze the shore as we steam in.

Now we have passed through the entrance. We are in a landlocked sea, upon which scores of little islands are seemingly floating, and in front of us, under the mighty hills, resting apparently upon the water, is the red-and-white city of Rio de Janeiro, looking at us through the masts of the steamers anchored in front of the town. Closer still, we see that the houses are of all shapes, sizes, and colors. They are roofed with red tiles, spotted with moss, and many of them are dirty with the moldy damp of old age.

Rio de Janeiro is one of the old cities of our hemisphere. It has grown up here because of its excellent harbor, and because it is situated at such a place that goods can be easily landed and carried by railroad to interior Brazil.

Let us stop a moment before going on shore, while I tell you its history. It is called Rio de Janeiro. It is always important to know just what names mean, for from the name of a place we can often learn something of its origin. It is so with Rio de Janeiro. This harbor was discovered just ten years after Columbus landed in America. At that time navigators from the different parts of Europe were sailing across the Atlantic to find out all about the New World.

Among them were two men named João Manoel and Amerigo Vespucci. They sailed down the coast of Brazil in 1501, and when they came by the sugar loaf into the bay where we now are they thought it was the mouth of a mighty river, so they called it Rio. The day that they came was the 1st of January, and the latter part of the name was supplied by the month—" River of January," Rio de Janeiro. It was afterwards discovered that it was not a river at all, for although about twenty small rivers flow down the mountains into the harbor, its waters are more an arm of the sea than the product of these little streams.

It was more than fifty years after this before the first settlement was made. About sixty-five years before the Pilgrim fathers crossed the Atlantic to Massachusetts, in order that they might establish a colony where they could worship God their own way, some French Huguenots emigrated to South America, for the same reason, and chose for their settlement one of the rocky islands of this harbor.

Here they lived for some time; but the Portuguese, who claimed all Brazil by right of discovery, made war upon them and finally drove them away. It was shortly after this that Rio de Janeiro was first started, but it was not made the capital of all Brazil until 1762.

The city at first was slow in growing. There were other cities, such as Bahia, farther north, which were much more important, and it was not until 1808 that the harbor was opened to the commerce of the world. When this was done ships from all parts of Europe began to land here, and the commerce which sprang up made Rio grow very fast.

Rio de Janeiro was for a long time the residence of the rulers sent by the King of Portugal to govern Brazil, and when in 1822 the Brazilians broke away from Portugal and declared their independence, much as we declared our independence of England in 1776, this place was kept as the capital.

Brazil did not at once become a republic. Its people thought they would prefer a monarchy, and they chose Dom Pedro I., one of the sons of the King of Portugal, as their ruler. He did not get along well with his subjects, however, and seeing that he could not reign peaceably, he said he would give up the throne if they would make his little boy their ruler in his stead.

The Brazilians agreed to do this, although little Dom Pedro II. was then only six years of age. The boy was declared emperor, and some of the best men were chosen to manage the government until he grew old enough to rule for himself. This time came when he reached sixteen, and from then on for forty-seven years he was the ruler of Brazil.

He made a good ruler, too, for he was just and kind, and anxious to do well for his people. But he had no son to succeed him, so in 1888 the Brazilians concluded they would change their government and become a republic. Dom Pedro was forced to resign, and a government much like ours was established.

It was decided at this time to keep the capital at Rio de Janeiro for the present, although the people are now considering whether it would not be better to choose another capital farther in the interior of the country.

During these different changes of government Rio de Janeiro has been steadily growing. It has increased very rapidly in population since Brazil was declared a republic, and it is now next to Buenos Aires the largest city in South America. It has seven hundred thousand people, and is a great commercial center.

"There is coffee everywhere."

We notice this as we land at the wharves among steamers from all parts of Europe. There are gangs of laborers, both negroes and whites, busy loading and unloading boats. Some of the ships taking on coffee are from Hamburg, Liverpool, and Lisbon, and others are loading for New York and Baltimore. There are also many steamers discharging all sorts of goods for Rio de Janeiro and the interior of Brazil.

Over there they are taking off a cargo of jerked meat which has come from the beef factories of Uruguay. The meat is in bags, and the men carry it out on their heads. Near by is a sailing vessel from New York filled with pine lumber, and next to it a ship which has thousands of boxes of kerosene made from petroleum which a short time ago was under the ground in our Pennsylvania oil regions.

Now we are off the ship and are pushing our way through the throng of workmen who are carrying the goods to the steamers. Most of them are negroes, and some are half naked. Nearly all of them carry burdens upon their heads. See those men who are bringing in the coffee bags from the wagons.

Each bag weighs as much as a man, but they trot along as though they were carrying feathers. They are in their bare feet, and we hear the thud, thud, thud, of their footsteps as they run to the steamer. Each man is paid a cent and a half per bag, and he is therefore anxious to carry as many bags as he can.

Now we have left the wharves and have entered the great coffee-exporting section of the city. There is coffee everywhere. The streets are walled with warehouses in which we see coffee piled up by the thousands of bags, and we can hardly get along the sidewalk for the men who are unloading the wagons. There are scores of half-naked men carrying the bags from the carts to the warehouses, and dozens of negro women down on their knees sweeping the stray coffee beans out of the cobblestones of the street that they may wash and sell them again. This building at our right is a coffee factory, and that hum is the noise of the machines which are cleaning the beans for the market. Next door is the office of one of the American exporting houses, which does nothing but ship coffee to New York, and farther on are the commission houses which buy coffee to sell to shippers.

Stop and listen to those knots of men on the street corners. They talk nothing but coffee. The very air smells of coffee, and we realize that we are in one of the great coffee ports of the world.

"They talk nothing but coffee."

We have already learned that the coffee crop is the most important crop of Brazil. The people make more money here in coffee than in anything else, and almost half of the coffee raised is sent to Rio de Janeiro to be shipped. Here also are the stores through which the coffee planters are supplied with goods, so that through coffee Rio de Janeiro has to a large extent become what it is.

After spending some time in the coffee section we take carriages for our hotel. Rio de Janeiro is too large a city to see in a day. It covers all together about nine square miles, extending from the harbor back to the hills. The streets go up hill and down. They cross one another at all sorts of angles, and we are unable to keep the points of the compass as we are whirled this way and that in going to the hotel.

XXXV. MORE ABOUT RIO.

WE shall take an interpreter with us this morning. The Spanish which we have learned in the South American capitals will be of little value in Rio de Janeiro, for the people here use Portuguese. Rio is the largest Portuguese-speaking city of the world. It has more people than all the cities of Portugal combined, and the country governed from it has a far greater population than the Portuguese-speaking population of the rest of the world.

We first drive rapidly over the city to get a general idea of its various features. It is far different from the other cities which we have visited. The streets are narrower, and the houses are taller and of a different shape. In some streets they are of three and four stories, and in the business sections we find that thousands of people live above the stores, having no yards, and taking their airing on the balconies which extend along the houses from story to story.

In the residence parts of the city the windows facing the

street are usually open, and out of nearly every window women and girls lean and stare at us as we go along. It seems to us that all the women of the city are at the windows, and our guide tells us that this is the chief occupation of the feminine part of the population. The better-class women seldom go out except to church. Their customs are much the same as those of the women of the Spanish-American cities.

The guide tells us that Brazilian girls do not associate with the young men, and that the girls of Rio are backward and bashful. We ask, if this is so, how it comes that they beckon, by crooking their fingers, to friends in the street cars which are passing, and that now and then they make motions to people over the way. He replies that these motions are mere salutations,—they mean " Good day," or " Good-by,"—and that the girls are only saluting their girl friends on the opposite side of the street or those who ride by in the cars.

We visit the business parts of the city. The stores are fine, and there are well-dressed men everywhere. Rio has many rich people, and the streets are thronged with buyers and sellers. Here we are in the Rua do Ouvidor (roo'a dō oo've-dor). This is the chief business street of Rio de Janeiro. It might be called the Broadway of the Brazilian metropolis.

What a queer street it is! It is not wider than one of our alleys, but it is walled with bright-colored three- and four-story buildings, which seem to lean toward each other as though to shut out the sun. From the first stories flagpoles extend out over the street so that they almost meet in the center, and between the poles are arches of iron gaspipes connecting the buildings and forming a canopy, as it were, over the Ouvidor.

Moving along under this canopy of poles and pipes is one of the strangest crowds of the world. There are people of all nations about us. We see the faces of Italians, Portuguese, Spaniards, French, Brazilians, and English. There are natty politicians dressed in black with tall hats, and there are merchants in business suits. There are Italian vegetable peddlers with baskets fastened to poles on their shoulders, and half-naked negro porters moving along with loads on their heads. There are bare-headed women and smartly dressed boys moving to and fro, forming all together such a human mixture as you will see nowhere else on earth.

Rio Peddlers.

Some of the people are shopping. Others have come to sell, and many to gossip and chat with their friends. The Ouvidor is Rio's great promenade, and many men meet their friends here instead of asking them to come to their houses.

Now we have left the Ouvidor and are passing through the side streets. What a lot of peddlers there are! Nearly all the hucksters of Rio carry their vegetables, fruits, and fish from house to house on their shoulders or upon their heads, instead of in carts or on donkeys. Here comes a man selling fish. He has his stock in two baskets fastened to the ends of a pole which rests on his shoulders. Behind him trots a man loaded down with long strings of onions. He has stopped at that house over there and is selling a string to the cook. The stems of the onions are so braided together with straw that they can be sold by the foot or yard. You may see stalls in the markets where only onions are sold.

But what is that squawking and crowing we hear in the next block? It comes from the wicker crate which that old negro woman is carrying on the top of her head. It contains three geese and four chickens. She is a chicken peddler, and she thus carries live fowls through the streets.

But here is another queer character. I mean that man on the opposite side of the street, who is clapping two sticks together. See the door opens and a woman asks him to enter. That man is a cloth peddler, his sticks are a part of his yard measure, and that clapping is the sign of his trade. Many of the women do not like to go to the stores, preferring to buy their goods of peddlers like him.

And so we go on meeting one odd character after another, now accosted by boys selling papers, and now by peddlers with candies and fruit. The strangest sights of all are the porters who carry huge loads on their heads. There goes one with a box on his crown which must weigh two hundred pounds. Behind him is a group of eight negroes who are moving along with a huge crate above them. Look closely and you will see inside the crate. It contains a piano, and they are carrying it on their heads from one part of the town to another.

Onion Stall in the Market.

But let us leave the business streets and visit the parks. We shall find them everywhere in and about the city, and shall know them by the royal palm trees which rise high above the rest of the vegetation and with quivering branches seem to wave us an invitation to enter. We are in the tropics, and the plants which we raise in our hothouses are to be found here growing wild.

"An avenue of royal palms."

We take a street car and ride for seven miles along the bay and by the residences of rich Brazilians to the Botanical Garden. This has plants and trees from all parts of Brazil. It has some of the most wonderful palm trees of the world. As we enter the gate we come into an avenue of royal palms, each of which is as tall as an eight-story house, although it is not more than a yard in diameter at the ground. There are more than a hundred of these magnificent trees lining the sides of the avenue. They rise in symmetrical shafts of silver gray, without a branch, for almost one hundred feet, and then shoot out into a canopy of fernlike green leaves. The avenue is not wider than an alley, and we seem to be walking between two files of giant soldiers, the plumes on their hats quivering in the breeze above us and almost shutting out the blue of the sky.

Crossing this avenue at right angles through the middle of the garden is another avenue of these same palm trees, and running from it here and there are gravel walks shaded by curious trees. We wander through groves of

"We wander through groves of feathery bamboos."

feathery bamboos, stalks of green cane fifty feet long, whose leaves interlock, forming a dense shade from the tropical sun. The bamboo groves are the favorite parts of the garden for picnics, and we see family parties sitting in them sipping their coffee.

We find here strange trees from all parts of the world. Here is a cinnamon tree, which grows perhaps best in the island of Ceylon. It has pale-yellow flowers, but its chief value is from the bark, which we use to flavor our pickles, and from which also comes cinnamon oil. That tree farther on is a clove tree. It is an evergreen, about twenty feet high, producing one of the spices of commerce. Then there are camphor trees and cork trees, and so many varieties of palms that we cannot describe them. There are all sorts of flowers, shrubs, and bushes. There are

"We go over ravines."

orchids of every variety, and great trees covered with blossoms. There are coffee plants of all sizes, and many tea shrubs, such as you see on the hillsides of China and Japan.

We might spend a long time in the Botanical Garden, but the hour for closing soon comes, and we take the cars again for our hotel. Later on we make tours over the little railroads which run from Rio de Janeiro up into the mountains. There are a number of such roads. Their tracks are just like those which take you to the top of Mount Washington and up to Pikes Peak.

Each track consists of two rails, with a ladderlike rail in the center. Upon this central rail moves a cogwheel attached to the engine, whose other wheels rest on the track. The engine is behind instead of in front of the train, and it puffs and puffs as it pushes us up the mountains through wonders of tropical scenery. We go over ravines hundreds of feet deep, and about mountain walls more than a thousand feet high. Now we seem to cling to the sides of the rock, and again great walls of rock hang over us, and we tremble as we think they might fall.

The air here is moist, and at times we are riding through clouds. As we go higher we have magnificent views of the city and harbor, and on the top of the Corcovado we stand upon a rocky peak, amid some of the grandest views of the world.

The great city of Rio and its beautiful harbor is just below us, but so far down that the houses look no bigger than dog kennels as they lie there skirting the water. The sea beyond has become a bed of sapphire under the rays of the sun, and upon it are rocky islands of curious shapes, while all about it rise mountain on mountain and hill upon hill.

See those four huge ocean steamers which are sailing in single file by the sugar loaf out to the sea. They look like canoes at this distance, but they are great ships loaded with coffee for Europe, New York, and New Zealand. The last one will pass down through the Strait of Magellan, and will go almost half around the world before it reaches its haven.

There are other fine views on our way to Petropolis, a

beautiful city of twenty-five thousand people, in the tops of the mountains just back of Rio. The region about it is so picturesque that it has been called the Switzerland of Brazil, and we shall find here the summer homes of many well-to-do Brazilians.

It is here that our minister to Brazil and the other foreign diplomats live. The city of Rio is often unhealthful.

Petropolis.

It has at times an epidemic of yellow fever, which is so bad for foreigners that of those who take it almost all die.

The air of the seacoast is hot and stuffy. We find it more bracing as the little cog engine pushes us on up the hills, and when we land in Petropolis we seem to be in a different world. We spend some days in wandering about through the mountains enjoying the scenery, and then go back to Rio and take ship for the north.

XXXVI. BAHIA AND THE DIAMOND MINES.

WE are in Bahia to-day. We have sailed three days north from Rio de Janeiro on our slow coasting steamer, and have come to anchor in the great Bay of San Salvador, under the bluffs on which most of the city is built. These bluffs rise almost straight up from the water, having only a narrow strip of land between them and the sea.

Upon this strip are the great wholesale importing and exporting houses, and upon the bluff are tall, bright-colored buildings, with feathery palms rising above them, quivering in the breeze. The bluff is so abrupt that elevators have been built to carry the people from one part of the town to the other, for it is very difficult to climb the

Bahia.

steep roadway which goes up the side of the hills. In the past sedan chairs were used, and those who could afford it were thus carried up on the shoulders of men.

As we look at Bahia from our ship it seems very large. It is the second city in size in Brazil, and one of great commercial importance. It is the capital of the second largest

Street Scene.

state of the country, and exports quantities of tobacco, cotton, and hides. It is a cultured city, and is noted for its hospitals and schools.

The Bay of San Salvador is about as large as that of Rio de Janeiro. There are more than a score of ocean steamers, numerous coasting ships, and a hundred small boats at anchor within it. There are many lighters or barges which are used to carry the goods between the steamers and the shore. All the craft have swung with the tide, and their noses are turned toward the city, so that we can easily imagine them a great naval fleet on its way to capture Bahia.

Bahia has had its share of invasions. It is one of the most interesting towns of South America historically, and is one of the oldest cities of Brazil. It had fifteen thousand people more than half a century before Boston was founded, and for two hundred years thereafter it was the capital of Brazil. It continued to be the chief city until coffee began to be raised in great quantities farther south, when Rio de Janeiro surpassed it.

The country about Bahia is so rich and the harbor so good that for many years some of the other nations of Europe coveted it. The Dutch took it several times and held it for years, and at one time it was besieged by the English.

Policeman.

It was for many years one of the chief centers for the slave trade of Brazil. It was one of the ports nearest Africa, and the negroes could be kidnaped and carried across the Atlantic into this bay. So many slaves were brought that in the year 1800 more than half the people of Brazil were slaves. A great many of the slaves who were brought to North America came to Bahia first, and indeed the slave trade went on secretly long after the rest of the world thought it was stopped.

This was not a long time ago, and as we land upon the wharves we notice that there are far more negroes than whites in the lower part of the city. Negro women sit upon the streets, with piles of fruit about them; negro men are loading and unloading the steamers, carrying huge bags and bundles on their heads; and in the narrow side streets little black babies, as naked as when they were born, are crawling over the cobblestones. There is a boy of eight who is playing horse. He has a little stick between his legs, and he is going on the gallop, although he has not a stitch on him.

"Each woman wears a turban."

How fat the women are! The negresses of Bahia are noted for their enormous size. Many of them weigh more than two hundred pounds, and their flesh fairly shakes as they carry themselves over the street. Each woman wears a turban of white or some gay color, and her dress is much like a long white nightgown with a deep lace edging at the shoulders, through the meshes of which you can see her black skin. This lace is a matter of pride with these women. Each makes her own lace, and the gowns of many are beautifully worked.

Some have gold bracelets on their arms and gold chains

about their necks, and we learn that many negroes have grown rich since they became free.

We find, as we continue our travels in Brazil, that the black man has here as many rights as the white man. Many of the white people have intermarried with the negroes, and there are millions of mulattoes in Brazil. The races are so intermingled that it is hard to tell who are pure whites or pure blacks.

Placer Mining.

Some of the negroes are very intelligent. During a visit to Brazil I found that the editor of one of the chief daily newspapers of Rio de Janeiro was a negro, and I was introduced to the archbishop of the province of Amazonas, whose face was as black as that of any African negro. There are colored men and women at almost every hotel table, and in the dining room of the steamers there are as many colored people at the table as whites.

We spend some time in Bahia visiting its cotton and tobacco factories. We see cartloads of hides and bales of goatskins brought in from the country. They are to be shipped to America to be made into shoes. We are told that the state of Bahia is rich agriculturally, and also that it has some of the best minerals of Brazil.

We are not accustomed to think of Brazil as a land of minerals. It has, however, gold, silver, iron, or coal in

"The mining is done in a rude way."

nearly every one of its states. Vast quantities of gold have been taken from Minas-Geraes (mē′näs-zhā-rä′ĕs), a state south of Bahia, and the placer mines of Bahia yield large golden nuggets. The mining is done in a rude way, the men digging the gravel up with hoes, and washing it out in the streams in bowls much like those we use to make bread.

The state of Bahia has the best diamond mines of

Brazil. It had for many years the richest diamond fields of the world, and it was noted for its precious stones until 1867, when the diamond fields of South Africa were discovered. Since then the best diamonds have come from Africa, although thousands of dollars' worth are still annually mined in Brazil.

The best diamond mines are far back of the city of Bahia, in the mountains at the head waters of the river Paraguacu. We go to them on boats and on mules; we can make but few miles a day, and it takes a long time.

The diamonds are found in the gravel which lies upon a bed of clay at the bottom of the river. The stream is quite deep, and the mining is usually done in the shallower places where there are not more than twenty feet of water, and where, owing to a bend in the river, the current is not strong.

A long pole is first driven down into the bed of the stream. Then two miners in a dugout canoe row out to the pole. One man remains in the boat, and the other, who is naked, dives down to the bottom. The diver has a big bag with him, the mouth of which is held open by an iron hoop. He rests the hoop on the river bed, and scrapes the gravel into the bag until he has filled it, when he climbs with it up the pole to the boat. The divers often remain under the water for more than a minute at a time.

Negro Woman of Bahia.

The bag of gravel is taken in the boat to the shore and emptied out upon the bank some distance back from the water, and the men then row back to the pole for more. This work goes steadily on through the dry season, for as soon as the rains begin the river gets so high that it is too deep to mine.

Then the men stop and wash over the gravel, looking carefully for diamonds and other valuable stones called carbons. Often many bushels of gravel must be handled before a diamond or a carbon is found.

The work is often very disappointing, and it requires great care and patience, but sometimes one little stone gives the miners a great reward for a whole season's work. When the mines were at their best only about one diamond a week was discovered, but the stones were so valuable that the few which were found brought for many years almost a million dollars a year.

The most of the diamonds now being discovered are small. They are shipped from the mines to Bahia, and from there sent to Europe to be cut into shape for jewelry, or for use in cutting glass or polishing gems.

The carbons are really impure or black diamonds. They are about as hard as a diamond, but are more porous. They are used for fine boring machines and for polishing very hard substances. They are found in all sizes, from little ones as small as a grain of sand to some which weigh hundreds of carats. A carat is a weight so small that it takes one hundred and fifty of them to make one ounce troy. It is the measure for diamonds and precious stones, and is therefore used for carbons. Not long ago carbons were selling for twenty dollars a carat, or so much that one large carbon which was recently found brought twenty thousand dollars.

XXXVII. ALONG THE COAST OF BRAZIL.

OUR travels of the next few weeks, comprised in this chapter, are along the coast of Brazil. We have taken a little Brazilian steamer at Bahia for Para, at the mouth of the Amazon. The distance looks quite short on the map, but it is more than two thousand miles, and as we move slowly along from city to city, stopping a day at each principal port to load and unload, it takes several weeks.

We first visit Maceo, the capital of the state of Algoas. This state lies between the San Francisco river and the state of Pernambuco. It is about as large as West Virginia, and is as thickly settled as Maine. The majority of its people are colored, and many of them are engaged in raising tobacco and cotton.

Maceo has about twenty-five thousand people. It is a city of one-story houses, built close to the streets and painted in the brightest of colors. Its houses are roofed with red tiles, and some are moss-grown with age. At the windows we see girls and women leaning out, just as we did in Rio de Janeiro, and, save that there are more negroes, the people look much the same.

Our next stop is at Pernambuco. This city is almost as large as Bahia. It is the capital of the state of Pernambuco, which produces vast quantities of sugar and cotton and the finest of goatskins and hides.

The proper name of the city is not Pernambuco, as it is often called, but Recife. The word "Recife" means reef, and this is the city of the reef. We see the reason for the name as we enter the harbor, which is formed by a great tongue of rock which here extends two or three miles out into the sea, making a tank or harbor not half a mile wide, but so deep that ocean steamers can come in and anchor. The rock extends out like a wall, and as we look at it we can hardly imagine that it was not all built

"The rock extends out like a wall."

by man. It does not rise very high above the level of the ocean, but so high that a low wall upon it suffices to prevent the waves from coming into the bay.

As we go in there is a heavy wind from the east, and the waves seem to gnash their teeth as they throw themselves against this stone wall, sending up masses of snow-white foam in their anger. Our ship has been rolling about on the ocean. Inside the harbor we lie perfectly quiet, and there is hardly a ripple, notwithstanding the billows outside. It is the first port at which the European steamers stop after leaving Lisbon, and more than one thousand ships call here every year,

We are now near a stone wharf, back of which are many great buildings filled with goods ready for shipment. A short distance above us are steamers taking on bales of cotton, and beside us is one unloading a cargo of dried beef from Montevideo.

We land, and, taking the street cars, are carried over one bridge after another. We go by horses loaded with cotton, carts pulled by oxen in shafts, and on into the city. Pernambuco has many canals, and its bridges remind us of Venice. It has many fine buildings. It has some

"The villages are of thatched huts."

stores and houses whose walls are faced with porcelain tiles imported from Europe. Its people pride themselves on their business ability, and it has indeed a great trade.

At Parahyba, still farther north, we have a chance to take a railroad ride into the interior during the waiting of the steamer. The train takes us for miles through groves of cocoanut palms. The vegetation is dense, and we see strange birds and strange animals in the trees. The parrots screech at us, and little monkeys, or marmosets, monkeys so small that you could put them into your pockets, scamper about through the branches.

The villages are of thatched huts with walls of mud or palm leaves. They have no glass windows, and the doors are of woven palm leaves, so light that they can be lifted away during the day. Naked children play about the streets, and half-naked black, brown, yellow, and white men and women stare at us as we go through.

Cotton Cart.

Most of the country is wild, and such farming as we see is done with the ax and the hoe. The ax is used to cut down the trees or bushes, after which the field is burned over, and the crops sown without plowing. In raising corn the grains are dropped upon the ground and covered. The soil is so rich that they quickly sprout, and after this it is necessary only to hoe down the weeds to produce a crop. Cotton is cultivated in much the same way. There is plenty of rain here, and everything grows well.

Farther back from the coast are the highlands of Brazil, and a little farther north, in the state of Ceara (sā-ä-rä′), at the port of which we next stop, the country is almost all high. It is a rolling country with mountain chains running through it, a part of the Brazilian highlands which is often subject to droughts.

When there is plenty of rain the crops are rich and everything is green and fresh, but during a long dry spell the land becomes as bare as the Desert of Sahara. Such times do not often occur, but when they do many of the people starve, and in the drought of 1877 and 1878 more than half of the whole population died of famine.

The port of Ceara often bears the name of Ceara on the map. Its Brazilian name is Fortaleza. It has one of the worst landing places on the east coast of South America. There is no pier, and we are carried from our boat to the shore in the arms of half-naked men, who charge us each eight cents a trip. The waves are rolling in on the beach as we walk through them suspended only a few inches above the water, and we tremble at what might happen if our bearers should slip on a stone.

"Here comes a water peddler."

The town of Fortaleza has about fifty thousand people. It is a beautiful city, with bright-colored houses, clean streets, and well-dressed people. We visit the market to learn what is raised in the country. We then take donkeys and ride through the city, and have time for a jaunt in the suburbs.

The street scenes are interesting, and every turn brings a new picture. We pass everywhere men and women carrying all sorts of things on their heads. There is a

Street Scene.

barefooted negress walking briskly along with a pumpkin balanced on the top of her head, and behind comes a boy carrying a two-bushel bag of flour in the same way. See, he has stopped there at that fence, and without lowering or touching his burden has lifted up his leg to the first board, and is industriously searching for something that is biting him.

Here comes a water peddler. He is driving a donkey, to the sides of which are slung four five-gallon casks. Behind him is a man with two horses, each of which carries a load of wood. The wood is fastened to the sides of the horses by wooden hooks made of forked limbs tied on like a pack saddle.

Do you see that cow over there with the milkman beside her, on his knees, squeezing the milk into a bucket? The calf stands behind; it is tied to its mother's tail with a rope. The calf has a muzzle upon it to keep it from feeding, and it thus goes along, tantalized by smelling and see-

In the Country.

ing the food which it cannot get at. That man is a milk peddler. He drives the cow from house to house and milks her to order. You would think that this would prevent his watering the milk. It does as a rule, but some milkmen, it is said, have water bags concealed in their shirts, with a pipe running down the sleeve to their hands, so that they can squeeze water in along with the milk.

Now we have left the city and are out in the country. We ride by banana fields, orange trees, and palm groves.

There is one palm tree which grows wild in this region which produces more things, perhaps, than any other tree in the world. This is the carnauba palm. Its trunk is used for rafters and building material, and from its roots is made a medicine like sarsaparilla. The small trees are used as vegetables, and from them wine and vinegar are made, as well as a starch like sago, and a kind of sugar. Its fruit is a good food for cattle, the pulp having an agreeable taste, and the nut is sometimes used as a substitute for coffee. The pith of this tree is as light as cork, and of the wood of the stem musical instruments are sometimes made.

Parrot Peddler.

When tapped the tree gives forth a white liquid much like the milk of a cocoanut, and of the strawlike bark, which grows on its trunk, hats, brooms, and baskets are made. The straw is also used for thatching houses. From the leaves a wax is obtained which is manufactured into candles, and which is extensively used in the states of northern Brazil. Ceara produces as much as two million pounds of this wax in a year.

Another thing for which Ceara is noted is its parrots. They are said to be among the best talking birds of the world. They are of a beautiful green-and-blue color, with a bit of red on the wings and neck, but are smaller than most other parrots. We are met in the markets by men carrying parrots, and they follow us down to our boat and beseech us to buy. We find we can get good ones for about two dollars apiece, but alas! they speak Portuguese, and before we can enjoy them they will have to be taught a new language. We take a number with us on the steamer, however, and amuse ourselves during the rest of our journey in giving the parrots lessons in elocution.

The weather grows warmer as we move farther north, stopping at one port after another. We sail along for almost a day only a little south of the equator, and anchor at last at the city of Para, in one of the mouths of the Amazon.

XXXVIII. THE VALLEY OF THE AMAZON, OR THE KING OF RIVERS.

BEFORE we begin our travels up the Amazon let us consider the wonderful region into which we are going. The Amazon is the king of rivers, and it flows through the greatest river valley of the world. It is indeed more like an inclined plane than a valley. Its width is about as great as the distance from New York to Salt Lake City. The hills slope down to it gradually on the north and south.

At its back are the great Andes, and from the foot of these it slopes downward toward the sea so gradually that in this long distance of about two thousand miles, or greater than the distance from New York to Denver, the fall is only two hundred feet. This is so little that, if the Amazon valley were free from trees and you and I were riding over it in a wagon, it would appear to be a level plain. The fall is only a little more than an inch to a mile.

The fall is so gentle that you would hardly think the

water would flow at all; but it does flow, and it goes in such a mighty volume that it carries with it vast quantities of the earth washings of the mountains. It would take millions of horses, working day and night, to haul down the mud which it is carrying into the Atlantic.

There is so much of this mud that for a day before we got to Para we were sailing through yellow water. In-

A Home on the Amazon.

deed, it is said that the waters of the ocean are stained by the mud five hundred miles from the mouth, and bits of tree trunks and vegetation from the Andes have been seen floating four hundred miles out in the ocean, having traveled almost as far from their homes in the mountains as the distance across our continent.

Is not this a wonderful river? How does it happen that it comes to be just where it is? What can be the cause of such a great volume of water, which can thus keep on flowing day and night, year in and year out, from one lifetime to another?

Let us see first how the Amazon valley was formed. Many geologists believe that there was here a great sea or strait joining the Atlantic and Pacific oceans. South America then consisted of two great divisions. On the north were the highlands of Guiana, Venezuela, and Colombia, and on the south were the highlands of Brazil and the remainder of South America, and between them the waters. Then there was a great upheaval of the earth at the westward. The Andes were thrown up out of the depths, and the basin of the strait was so raised that the waters flowed down into the Atlantic, and the Amazon valley was formed.

So the salt waters were taken away. Now let us see whence this perpetual flow of fresh water comes. It is brought here by the trade winds, which fill themselves full of water as they cross the Atlantic. They are loaded when they reach the coast of Brazil, and they sweep up the wide trough of the Amazon valley, dropping their rain as they rise and cool in their journey to the mountains. They drop more and more as they go to the westward, and the water falling over this vast surface is carried by countless streams into the trough known as the Amazon river. So much water falls that the Amazon valley is perhaps the rainiest region of the world. There is so much rain, indeed, that if the mouth of the river could be dammed up by a great dike a vast sea would soon be formed.

It is estimated that so much rain falls that if it did not flow off, and remained where it fell, the vast valley would be so covered with water in a single year that the tallest man could drown anywhere in it. The average rainfall is seventy-two inches per annum, and where we are now enough rain falls every year to cover the ground with water to the depth of a fifteen-story house.

Exploring the Amazon.

As we stand on the deck of the steamer we notice that the air is full of moisture. Para has a heavy rain almost every afternoon, and its people make their appointments to call after the daily shower. We shall find the air moist all the way up to the Andes, and we must take out our knives, cameras, and guns every day or so and clean them. The air is so wet that anything steel will rust in your pockets, and a gun loaded overnight will be so damp that it will not go off in the morning. We must not be surprised to find little moldy spots on our black shoes when we get up, and such of us as are carrying photographic materials had better seal them up in tins, for the dampness will spoil them.

We are, fortunately, on the Amazon when the water is low. The great river for almost two thousand miles from the sea is now only from two to five miles in width. During the rainy seasons of November and February it rises and slowly climbs up to from thirty to fifty feet above its present level. At such times it floods much of this low valley, and thousands of square miles are for months covered with water. The river then flows in and out among the tops of the trees, and the valley for a thousand miles back from the Atlantic is a great inland sea from fifteen to one hundred miles wide. In the dry times you may see vast stretches of meadows which are made by such floods, where the water lies for months upon the land, so long that the trees will not grow upon it. The result is the pasture fields of the Amazon, which at times of flood are vast lakes.

The most of the valley, however, is a forest, in which there are no paths, and through which we can go only upon the streams in canoes or boats. There are so many streams, however, that the most of the forest can be reached by water. The Amazon in its long course receives more than one hundred rivers, into which flow a myriad of brooks. Of its rivers eight are said each to have a navigable length of more than one thousand miles. Up these rivers you can go on the north until you are very close to the head waters of the Orinoco—so close that you could carry your boat and go down in it to the Atlantic Ocean. On the south you could sail up the Tapajos so far that, with a very short trip, you could drag your canoe into the tributaries of the Paraguay and Parana.

The Amazon system is unquestionably the greatest upon the globe, and the river itself will surprise us more as we travel upon it. We shall go in a big ocean steamer to Manaos (mä-nä′ōs), on the Rio Negro, and we may

An Amazon Alligator.

there take smaller steamers which will carry us on the Amazon to Iquitos, Peru, more than twenty-three hundred miles from the Atlantic.

If the Hudson river, which empties into the Atlantic at New York, were a great stream flowing through our continent from the west, so that we could enter it and sail clear across the land to Salt Lake City on a steamer, we should have about the same condition of transportation as prevails on the Amazon. We might indeed almost cross the continent by water, for the Pacific is not very many miles from Iquitos. We could hire mules there and thus make our way over the Andes to the coast.

XXXIX. PARA, THE METROPOLIS OF THE AMAZON.

BEFORE we start on our tour up the Amazon we must explore the city of Para. It lies in front of us, back of the masts of those sailing vessels and steamers lining the shore. There is a row of tall palms between it and the river. They rise high above that line of white and bright-colored houses, and their quivering branches are swaying in the wind from the sea.

The city seems small, but the land is so low that we can see but little of it from the steamer. It runs far back from the water. It is as large as Indianapolis, and has a vast trade with all parts of the Amazon valley. The ships among which we are moving have come from far up the river. There is a side-wheel steamer which has a load of manioc and cacao from the Madeira. It has brought it more than a thousand miles to Para. That ship beside it, with the canvas over its deck, under which are numerous hammocks in which people are lying, is about to start up the Tocantins river, and that boat filled with rubber has been floated down from the wilds of Bolivia.

See that steamer over there with the English flag flying from its mast. It is loaded for Liverpool. The great vessel beside it, with the dense smoke pouring from its funnel, is a Portuguese ship starting out for Lisbon, and farther over you may see a big cargo steamer just in from New York. It has brought down kerosene, hardware, pine lumber, and codfish to be sold in Para, and it will carry back great boxes of rubber to be used in our factories.

What a busy stream it is through which we move as we

go to the wharf! We pass hundreds of sailboats filled with vegetables and fruit, and countless dugouts being paddled swiftly along toward the shore. Now we are at the landing, and the cargadores begin to load and unload the steamer. They work in their bare feet, carrying the

Wharves at Para.

goods in and out of the ship on their heads. Their faces are of all shades of white, brown, and black. Among them are negroes from Jamaica, and Spaniards, Portuguese, and mulattoes from all parts of Brazil.

We push our way through them and walk on into the business sections of Para. The buildings are of three or four stories. They are built close to the sidewalks along narrow streets, and their walls are of all colors, some being faced with blue, yellow, and green porcelain tiles.

How big the shops are! They have large stocks of

goods, some piled upon the pavements outside the storerooms. That block over there is chiefly filled with dry-goods establishments. See the bright-colored calicoes and white cottons which hang on the walls outside the shops, and among them the numerous hammocks. The hammocks are of all grades and all prices. Some are a

"How big the shops are!"

lacework of fine threads, and others are mere strips of canvas. Hammocks are the beds of the Amazon valley, and we must buy some before we go up the river.

We shall need them to sit in by day, and in many places they will serve us as our beds at night. There are places on the boats in which hammocks can be swung, and in our camps in the woods the branches of the trees will serve for support. We are now in the tropics, and shall find hammocks much cooler than beds. They are also much safer, for the bugs, ants, and snakes cannot crawl into them so easily as they could into a bed.

We take the street cars and ride through one business block after another, realizing as we do so the immense trade of Para. We go by beautiful parks, filled with palms and other tropical trees, and on into streets well shaded, past the homes of the rich Paranese. The houses

Along the River, Para.

here are fine. The windows are filled with women and girls looking out. Some sit and lean on the sills, and others, beautifully dressed in silk gowns, hold in their arms naked babies. Soon we reach the edge of the city and come to the dense forest out of which Para has been cut.

We walk a few blocks, and return to the wharf through a different section of the city. We stop at that part of the river where fruits, vegetables, and merchandise are brought from the neighboring islands in small boats. The scene here is a bright one. There are scores of gayly dressed negro women peddling all sorts of things. There are women and men trotting along with great burdens on their heads, and people of all classes buying and selling fish, fruit, and vegetables, and some queer merchandise.

Banana Market.

See that great pile of baskets which has just been brought in from the boats. They look like round peach baskets and are lined and covered with green palm leaves. A crowd has gathered about them, and the people are buying them and carrying them off on their heads. What can they be? Let us open a basket and see. We lift up the palm leaves and find that it is filled with coarse meal; it is white, and it looks much like ground popcorn. We taste it. It makes us think of sawdust. It is manioc flour, an article which forms the food of the people of a great part of Brazil. It is very nutritious. Indeed, we consume great quantities of manioc ourselves, for it is from it that the tapioca which we use in soups and puddings is made. From the wharves we go to the markets. The fruits remind us of Ecuador, and show us that we are again in the lands of the equator. We buy delicious pineapples and cocoanuts for a few cents apiece, and the bananas and oranges are so ripe that they almost melt in our mouths. There are quantities of black tobacco in long twists, some as big around as a baseball bat; and peddlers bring us parrots and monkeys and ask us to buy.

"We see many vultures."

In the market we see many vultures. They sit on the roofs about the court, ready to swoop down and eat up the scraps of meat thrown away by the butchers. Vultures are the scavengers of the Amazon, and are never killed by the people. They are quite tame, and if they were not so disgusting we might easily catch them and pet them.

But what is that on the head of the man who is going out of the door of the market house? It is as big around as a washtub and about a foot thick. See, it is alive! It is a turtle which is lying upon its back; it is poking its head in and out of its shell as the man carries it off. That is one of the big turtles of the Amazon. They are found near Para, and exist in large quantities in most parts of the

"See it is alive!"

Amazon basin. They have their breeding places, where they go in countless numbers at certain times of the year. They dig holes in the sand and lay their eggs there. The eggs are about as big as hens' eggs, and have a leathery skin instead of a shell. Each turtle lays about one hundred and twenty eggs, and millions upon millions are deposited in these laying places.

The people learn where they are. They go to them in crowds and dig up the eggs, and use them to make turtle oil or turtle butter. The yolks of the eggs contain much oil. The egg hunters fill their canoes with the eggs and then pound them to a jelly with sticks, or tread them into

Street in Para.

a mush with their feet. After this some water is poured into the mixture, and it is allowed to stand in the sun. In a short time the oil rises to the surface. It is skimmed off and further purified by being boiled in copper kettles. It is used largely for burning and sometimes for cooking.

While hunting the eggs many little turtles are caught. These are esteemed great delicacies. They are sold by dozens in strings. We see many in the markets, and find that they are delicious when roasted.

XL. IN THE LAND OF RUBBER.

OUR travels during the next few days shall be devoted to the rubber industry of the Amazon valley. Para is the chief rubber port of the world, and in its warehouses we can see how rubber is packed for the markets. There are many rubber trees in the forests which grow on the islands near the mouth of the Amazon. These islands we can reach by a steam launch, and we have arranged to visit a rubber plantation.

But first let me tell you a little about this wonderful product. Rubber has now become one of the most important materials used by man. A century ago it was not known as being of value except for rubbing out pencil marks. Now it is used in many kinds of machinery. It keeps us dry in wet weather, and in the cities even the horses have rubber coats. We ride over the streets on rubber tires. We wade through the wet in rubber boots, and race horses are shod with rubber shoes. During one year the public school children of New York used more than five tons of rubber ink erasers, and rubber bands are consumed by the million in our large business cities. There are indeed so many uses for rubber that we cannot enumerate them; so many that rubber grows more and more costly every year, and the business of gathering it increases.

The best rubber, and indeed the most of the good rubber, comes from the Amazon valley. It is made from the sap of the *Siphonia elastica*, a forest tree which grows wild in this region. It is found scattered over a district as large as all the United States east of the Mississippi river, extending from the mouth of the Amazon westward to the wilds of Peru, and on the south running far down into Bolivia and Matto Grosso, Brazil.

The rubber tree flourishes best in land which is flooded during part of the year. Ground which is always above water, or which has not good drainage, will not do for it. The very best conditions for the growth of such trees exist south of the Amazon, and also upon the islands and lowlands not far from its mouth.

The trees from which the rubber now comes are not

cultivated. They might be and probably will be raised on plantations when the wild trees are worn out and the demand for rubber increases. Each rubber tree bears many seeds. Its fruit is like a horse-chestnut, three seeds being found in each shell. When it is ripe the shell bursts with a noise like a firecracker and throws the nuts to some distance. There are so many nuts on each tree that it is said a man could easily gather enough in a day to plant a hundred acres of land. The seeds after planting grow rapidly. They must have plenty of moisture and heat, but must be shaded from the direct rays of the sun. After a time they can be transplanted, and if set out in the right soil they will thrive without cultivation.

It takes from fifteen to twenty years, however, before the trees will produce enough rubber sap to pay the proprietor, and this is so long that at present the people prefer to hunt for and tap the wild trees. There are thousands of men doing this in the different parts of the Amazon valley. In some places Indians are employed to gather the rubber, and there are rubber camps thousands of miles inland from where we now are. Indeed, some of the rubber which is shipped from Para has to travel as far in getting to that port as it does in going from Para to New York.

Our steam launch leaves Para in the evening, and we spend all night upon the Amazon. How bright the stars are, and how the moon shines here in the soft air of the tropics! Our hammocks are slung from the roof of the boat, and the warm wind from the ocean fans us to sleep. We ride all night through one narrow channel after another, and when we awake we are at the house of a rubber planter. A little wharf made of wood extends from his front door out into the river, and as we step out of the boat we are within a few yards of the house. It is a low, one-story building, roofed with red tiles, with a wide veranda about it. At one end is a storeroom filled with the groceries and dry goods which the planter sells to his rubber gatherers, and on the veranda itself are piles of what look like smoked hams, but which are really lumps of rubber ready to be shipped to market. The planter gives us a breakfast of coffee and rolls, and later we walk with him through the dense forest, winding our way this way and that from one rubber tree to another.

How interesting it is, and how different from what we imagined! We have heard of rubber groves and rubber forests. There is no such thing in nature. The trees are widely scattered. They are so far apart that each man has to walk several miles in gathering his sap for the day. Each man has his own trees to attend to, ranging from sixty to one hundred and fifty trees, according to the distance between them, and this number is called a path or road. The size of a rubber plantation is estimated by the number of paths or roads it contains. The roads are mere footpaths which lead through the forest from one rubber tree to another.

We are winding our way along such a path now. Let us stop at one of the trees and look at it. It is different from the other trees about it, but it is not at all like the rubber trees or plants which we have in our hothouses. They are lean plants with enormous, thick leaves of smooth, polished green.

That rubber tree there has a trunk as big around as your waist. It is a great forest tree, and its leaves are somewhat like those of the English ash. Look up and see how smooth the bark is. It is of a whitish gray, and at a distance of twelve feet above the ground it shines almost like silver. Farther down it is scarred, black, and warty, with streaks of yellow matter here and there in the bark, as if melted beeswax had been poured upon it. Take out your knife and dig up a bit of the wax, so you can catch hold of it. Now pull at it. You can stretch it from six inches to a foot from the tree before it comes off. That is coarse rubber, the remains of the sap which has dried on the tree. It will all be pulled out and saved, although it will be sold at a much lower price than the better varieties which we shall see made later on.

Tapping a Rubber Tree.

But here comes the rubber gatherer to tap the tree for the day. He has a little tomahawk, or hatchet, the blade of which is just about an inch wide, and a lot of tin cups of the size of an egg cup. With the hatchet he makes a gash in the bark, just deep enough to go through without cutting the wood. As he pulls back the hatchet a white fluid begins to ooze out. It is just like milk, and makes us think of the juice of the milkweed. The fluid comes out in great drops, and the man takes one of the little tin cups and fastens it into the tree just under the wound, so that the milk drops down into the cup. He now makes two or three other gashes in the tree, fitting each gash with its cup, and then goes on to the next. He continues his work until every tree in his path has been tapped.

Collecting Rubber Sap.

The proprietor shows us how slowly the sap runs. He tells us that only a few tablespoonfuls can be gathered from each wound in a day. The sap flows best in the morning, and it is along about noon that the rubber man comes back to empty the milk out into a gourd or bucket. The amount collected varies according to the richness of the trees, but if a man can gather two quarts of milk in one day from his path he thinks he has done very well.

The next process is turning the milky sap into the rubber of commerce. This is very important. The sap coagulates, or becomes hard, upon exposure to the air, and if it is not properly treated it turns to coarse rubber and must be sold for low prices. The fine rubber is cured by smoking, and the best rubber comes from the sap which is smoked a few hours after it is gathered. Our planter makes very fine rubber, and his men are required to cure their rubber sap as soon as they return from the forest.

Smoking the Sap.

There goes a man now with a bucket containing two quarts of sap which he has just brought from the trees. Let us follow him and see the process of curing. We go with him to an open shed, and watch him pour the sap into a great bowl as large as those we use in mixing bread. See how white the sap is! It looks just like milk. It tastes sweet, and is so thin that you could easily drink it.

Now the man stoops down and builds a fire of palm nuts in one corner of the hut under a clay chimney raised a little from the floor. The chimney is so small that its top does not reach so high as our waists. See how the nuts burn, and watch that dense smoke which pours out through the chimney.

Notice the man. He has taken a long paddle and thrust the end of it into the milk. It comes out as white as snow. The milk has stuck to the paddle. The man now thrusts the end of the paddle into the smoke, twisting it rapidly about as he does so, so that no drop of the precious sap may fall into the fire.

Rubber Gatherers.

As the smoke touches it the rubber thickens and hardens; its white becomes streaked with brown by the smoke. It has soon coated the paddle like varnish. Now the man thrusts the paddle again into the milk bowl. When he brings it out there is a fresh coat of rubber sap on it ready for smoking. This is hardened in the same way, and the man so continues until he has built up about the end of the paddle a mass of rubber as large as a six-pound ham. Now he takes a knife and makes a cut in one side. He pulls off the rubber and carries it to the house, where it is piled up with other lumps for shipment to Para, and thence to factories all over the world.

After dinner the planter tells us that he will return to Para with us if we will allow him to tie his boat to our launch. We gladly consent, and our little steamboat takes not only the boat, but a big shipment of rubber. The rubber hams are carried by men down the wharf and piled up in the boat. There are hundreds of them, and the boatload represents a vast deal of money.

Good rubber is worth so much that a lump as big as a baseball will sell for a dollar. The rubber has to be carefully handled. When one of the hams falls on the wharf it bounces high up into the air and rolls about so that we laugh when we see the men trying to catch it again.

At Para our load of rubber is put into carts and carried to one of the great warehouses for shipment. The buyers look each piece carefully over. They cut it in two to see that the rubber is pure all the way through. They weigh it and pack it up in great pine boxes, each of which holds between three and four hundred pounds. In such boxes it is shipped to the United States and to Europe.

XLI. A TRIP ON THE AMAZON.

OUR next trip is to be up the Amazon. We shall travel several weeks on the river, but we might spend years and not see all of its wonders. Lying in our hammocks on the deck of the steamer, we float for miles out and in between walls of forest trees a hundred feet high. Now we are close to one bank of the river, and now we have crossed and are traveling near the dense vegetation of the opposite side. At times we go for miles in midstream, where the river is so wide that the forests make two faint lines of blue on the right and left. Now we are steaming out and in between islands so close to the land that we can see into the huts of the rubber gatherers and others who have made their rude homes on the banks of the river.

We are passing one on the right. It is not more than fifteen feet square. It is a rude hut thatched with palm leaves, with holes in the walls for windows. There is a shed at one side, and in this there are two hammocks, in each of which a woman is lying. We see other huts farther on. Each hut has its boats tied to the shore. The owners rush to the banks and pull up the boats at the approach of the steamer. Sometimes they jump into them and row out from the land to prevent the waves made by the ship from overturning their boats or filling them with water.

The most of the boats are dugouts, although at the larger houses there are rowboats, some of which are painted in bright colors. It is only by boats that the people can go from one place to another. There are no roads through the dense forests of the Amazon. Each hut has a little clearing about it, but there are few open spaces which are more than an acre in size, except farther up where the cacao trees have been planted, and in the pastures made by the floods of which we have already learned.

We have often heard of the tropical forest. We find it interesting, but far different from what we supposed. It is not a great mass of palm trees. Most of it is made up of giant forest trees, not unlike some we have in the temperate zone, and as we steam up the river a mile or so from the shore, it looks just like our forests at home. As we get closer, however, we see here and there the broad leaves of the palms shining against the lighter green of other trees.

There are hundreds of feathery creepers, air plants, which hang like strands of green silk down from the branches of these great forest giants. There is a dead limb clothed with orchids. Farther over a great round mass of blue flowers rises out of the green. That is a tree in blossom, and if you look to the right you may see other vast bunches of white, yellow, and purple, the flowers of other forest trees which grow only along the Amazon. There are trees here, as tall as the tallest trees of our forests, each of whose tops forms a bouquet of violet blue as big as a haystack. They rise, surrounded by green, a hundred feet above us. There are stacks of buttercups away up in the air, and we now and then see trees loaded with flowers much like tiger lilies, only they have a tinge of red mixed with their yellow and black, which makes them more beautiful.

Close to the shore in many places the trees rise like a wall up from the water. Many of them are a hundred feet high, and the creepers and vines which crawl up their trunks and wind this way and that in a tangled mass are so thick that it is almost impossible to cut your way through them. The bark of most of the trees is of a whitish gray. Some of the trunks are so twisted and ribbed that they look like mighty cables of white taffy which have been braided together to support the vast mass of foliage above them.

One of the noblest trees of all rises high above the

others. This is the tree which produces the Brazil nut. It grows to a height of one hundred and fifty feet, with magnificent foliage of large dark-green leaves. Its fruit is of the shape of our black walnut, save that it is larger around than the largest baseball. It has an outer skin like a walnut, with a similar hard shell within, and inside the hard shell are the long, three-cornered Brazil nuts which are sold in the stores. There are often twenty nuts in one

On the Rio Negro.

shell. The nuts are gathered and carried in boats to Para, where the shells are broken and the Brazil nuts of commerce taken out. The nuts are quite heavy, and we tremble when we get off now and then at a landing and walk under the trees, for fear some may drop on our heads. We hear monkeys chattering in the branches, and fear that they may throw the nuts at us from the tops of the trees.

We see also the trees that produce the sapucai'a nut. This is almost as big as a football. It is of the shape of an urn with a nicely fitting lid. When it is ripe the lid falls off and the nuts within drop out.

The channel of the Amazon is very wide for a long distance from its mouth. At the town of Obidos (o-be'dōs), five hundred miles from the Atlantic, it narrows, and its immense volume pours through a channel about a mile wide. The current here is so strong that our steamer does not rely on its anchor alone, but has also a cable by which it is tied to a tree on the bank. We wait for some hours, and during the stay are taken in canoes to the shore. The town is a collection of rude houses built along three or four narrow streets.

Obidos has a factory for making chocolate, and we learn that there are many cacao plantations near by. We see more cacao trees as we sail on our way up the river. The orchards line the south bank of the Amazon for miles.

The cacao trees are about twenty feet high. They branch up in sprouts from the bottom. Some of them are loaded with what look like small melons or squashes. This is the cacao fruit, inside of which are the seeds which form the cacao bean of commerce. They are just like the beans which we saw in Ecuador and Colombia, and the trees are just the same. The cacao of the Amazon is said to make excellent chocolate. About half a million dollars' worth of it is shipped from Para every year, and the product all told amounts to thousands of tons.

We pass the mouth of the Madeira some distance above Obidos, and soon after this come to a place where the waters of the Amazon and the Rio Negro meet. Those of the Rio Negro are as black as ink, and those of the Amazon as yellow as mud.

TRIP ON THE AMAZON. 325

The Rio Negro keeps its color for a long distance after it reaches the Amazon before it is swallowed up by that great yellow monster. We ride along in our steamer on the line where the two colors join, seeing black on one

Indians, Northern Brazil.

side of the ship and yellow on the other, but soon turn to the right and sail for an hour up the wide Rio Negro, when we reach the city of Manaos, the metropolis of northern Brazil.

Manaos lies on the river bank high above the water, its wide streets lined with palm trees, and its bright houses shining out under the tropical sun. It is a large city for this part of the world. It has about half as many people as Para, and, as the center of the interior trade of the Amazon valley, it must continue to grow.

We are surprised to find good houses and modern improvements here in the heart of the continent. Manaos has electric street cars, electric lights, and good schools. It has one of the finest theaters of Brazil, a great market, a museum, and some very large stores. To it come steamers from all parts of the Amazon valley, and the river is so deep to this point that the largest ocean steamers go from Manaos to New York and Europe.

The rubber gatherers bring quantities of rubber to Manaos from the vast regions west and south of it, and they come by the hundreds here for their supplies, often

Wharves, Manaos.

trading rubber for goods. It is from here that expeditions start out to explore the unknown wilds of the Amazon and its tributaries, and we can find here boats and men who will go with us to almost any part of this unknown region.

We could take a steamer and sail more than thirteen

hundred miles farther west into Peru, and there find a trail which would bring us over the Andes to the west coast, or we might go by another steamer down the Madeira, and by walking about its great falls reach the Beni and travel to a point from where we could easily get back to La Paz, Bolivia, or Lake Titicaca.

We decide, however, to continue our journey up the Rio Negro. We ride for days through its black, muddy waters, winding in and out through the dense forests, until we come to the mouth of the Cassiquiari (kä-sē-kē-ä′rē) river, a stream which unites the Orinoco with the Amazon system. We move northward on the Cassiquiari, and are soon floating down the Orinoco on our way to the Atlantic.

XLII. ON THE ORINOCO AND THE LLANOS.

IS not this a wonderful river system by which we can come from the Amazon into the Orinoco without traveling upon land? We have seen how close the head waters of the Paraguay river are to the southern tributaries of the Amazon. Indeed, with a short canal, we might start from the Atlantic into the mouth of the Orinoco, and go on the water clear through interior South America, coming out again into the Atlantic through the Rio de la Plata. We saw something of this as we came up the Amazon, but if you will take your map you will see how easily it could be done.

First trace your way from the Orinoco into the Cassiquiari, then go over the route we have just come down to the mouth of the Tapajos, and sail up this to its source. You are now so near the beginnings of the Parana system that in a day you could walk to some of them, and you would have then but to float with the current down the route up which we came in visiting Matto Grosso, Brazil.

We are now on the Orinoco. Its thick yellow waters are loaded with sediment. They are rushing in a swift current down to the Atlantic. They have been gathered from the mountains far to the westward. They have been poured in through countless branches from the llanos, or vast meadows, and other parts of the basin, a territory one seventh as large as the whole United States.

The Orinoco is indeed a wonderful river. It is the third largest river on the South American continent, being surpassed only by the Amazon and the La Plata. It is almost fifteen hundred miles long, and its main stream is navigable for twelve hundred miles. It has four hundred navigable branches, and it so drains this vast region that there are few places in its basin where you cannot reach navigable water by a mule ride of a few days.

Now we have left our small boats and are again on a large steamer. We are traveling through a country far different from that of the Amazon. The dense forest has disappeared, and a vast expanse of plain stretches away on both sides of the river. The plains are covered with coarse grass, the most of which is now luxuriantly green. Here and there it is gray, and we sometimes pass a tract which has been blackened by fire.

See that smoke away off to the right, and the flames rolling up from the ground. That is one of the prairie fires of the llanos of central Venezuela. It has been started by the farmers. They are burning off the dead grass that the green sprouts may more quickly come up.

What a lot of cattle there are on the plains! We see herds of thousands, and we learn that cattle raising is one of the great industries of this country. More and more cattle are being raised every year, and Venezuela now has several million beeves feeding upon its great plains. The beasts are grown for their meat and their skins. The

Indian Village.

skins are salted and dried, and are shipped by the thousands to the United States and Europe, where they are tanned and made into shoes and other such things.

The meat is stripped off in sheets from the bones; it is salted and made into jerked beef, which is so much desired by the people of Spanish and Portuguese America. It is taken on the steamers down the Orinoco, and has a ready sale in the various islands of the West Indies.

But what is that town we see away off on the right bank of the river? There are blue-and-white buildings with red roofs rising in terraces upon the low hills. There are steamers at anchor at the wharf, and the place seems quite a city. It is the first evidence of civilization we have seen since we left Manaos some weeks ago. That is the chief city of interior Venezuela, the metropolis of

Group of Natives.

the llanos. Its name is Ciudad Bolivar (sē-ū-däd' bō-lē'-var). It has perhaps ten thousand people, and it forms the center of trade for a vast region. From it go the chief exports of cattle, and it is also the point from which expeditions start out for the gold mines farther south.

Now we are in front of the town. We have landed and are walking up steep, narrow streets paved with rough cobbles. The houses are almost all of one story. They are built about courts, and they seem like those of the Spanish towns we saw in our tour along the west coast. There is plenty of grass in the streets, and we look about in vain for a carriage. There are no wheeled vehicles to speak of. We shall have to use horses in making our trips into the country. Every well-to-do family on the llanos

"Things are carried about upon donkeys."

has plenty of horses. The stock is especially fine. The horses are of Moorish breed. They have a gait like a pace, which carries you along so gently that you feel you might be riding on the rocking-horse used by your baby brother.

There are few carts anywhere in Venezuela. Things are carried about upon donkeys. There comes one now with two huge baskets filled with vegetables slung to his sides. Behind him is another carrying boxes of bread, and we see others loaded with all sorts of things, including wood, bricks, and stone, which they are patiently bearing to different parts of the city.

We see many donkeys which have come in from the country when we visit the market. They have neither

La Guaira.

bridles nor halters, and they stand blinking their eyes, patiently waiting for their masters to drive them back home. Some are hobbled by ropes tied about their front legs, and not a few are moving along by lifting their two front feet at one time, to get the vegetables and scraps which have dropped from the loads of other beasts going by.

We find in the market many interesting things. There

ON THE ORINOCO. 333

are all sorts of vegetables and tropical fruits. There are quantities of plantains and bananas, which, we learn, form a large part of the food of the people. There is plenty of beef, and manioc flour such as we saw on the Amazon.

There are red clay bowls sold for cooking, and many grass hammocks. Hammocks are used as beds by nine tenths of the people, and they form for almost all the loafing and sitting places during the day. We frequently sleep in hammocks during our visits to the large farmers near Ciudad Bolivar.

Even the wealthiest people have country houses built of poles and mud, which are rude in the extreme. They have large verandas about them, and in this warm region the veranda is the pleasantest part of the house. We spend hours upon it during the heat of the day, and it is there that we often come to sleep for the night, preferring its cool air to the heat of our bedrooms.

There are steamers every few days from Ciudad Bolivar down the Orinoco. They sail out through the delta, and go on to Trinidad, one of the West India Islands, from where you can get ships for La Guaira and other coast cities of Venezuela.

It is upon one of these steamers that we sail down the river. Our boat is a great side-wheel steamer with two decks, much like the boats on the Hudson. It has an American captain, but the passengers, with the exception of ourselves, are all Venezuelans. Some of them are white, others are of the mixed race formed by the union of the Spaniards and Indians, and others seem to have negro blood in their veins. We have a few native Indians among the deck passengers, and there are a number of priests, dressed in the big hats and long gowns of their class. We have many women and children, who have with them such a lot of cats, dogs, monkeys, parrots, and other birds, that the scene on the deck makes us think of a little zoölogical garden.

We steam for two days before we come to the delta. The river is wide, and there are numerous islands. There are few villages and not many people. The water of the river is so thick that we seem almost to see it drop mud as it flows. From it has been built up the great delta through which we pass out on our way to the sea.

The delta of the Orinoco is about as large as the State of New Jersey. It has flowing through it many deep channels, which are lined with a tropical jungle. There are mango trees and palms, bananas and wild forest trees, bound together with long creepers, or lianas, much like those we saw on the Amazon.

We see Indian huts and clearings which have here and there been made in the jungle. The huts are made of poles and palm leaves, and the people within them lie in their hammocks or stand outside and gaze at us as the steamer goes by. The men and boys have only a rag about the waist, and the little children are naked. The women wear short petticoats made of the fibrous bark of the palm tree. All seem lazy and worthless, and we learn that they hunt and fish only enough to keep them alive.

XLIII. VENEZUELA AND ITS CAPITAL.

SHORTLY after leaving the delta of the Orinoco we reach the island of Trinidad, where we stay but a few hours, and then take ship for the ports of Venezuela. We travel from one place to another, making excursions back into the country, visiting all the large cities, and spending some weeks in Caracas the capital.

Venezuela is a very large country. We see that it has vast tracts of rich land, and realize that it is one of the best of the South American republics. Its territory is so large that if it could be transported to the United States it would cover all Colorado, Texas, Idaho, and California. It is greater in extent than Germany and France combined, and large parts of it have excellent soil. We have already seen the rich pastures of the south.

There are few countries of the world which are so well watered. We know something of the Orinoco system. Venezuela has many other navigable rivers. It has, all told, more than one thousand streams. Upon its coast there are thirty-two harbors and numerous bays. The largest bay is Lake Maracaibo, the area of which is about the size of our Great Salt Lake.

It was from Lake Maracaibo that Venezuela got its name. When the Spaniards discovered the country, about eight years after Columbus first came to America, they entered this bay. On some of its shores and islands they found a tribe of natives living in huts, made of palm leaves and rushes, built upon piles which they had driven down into the sand. Their huts were surrounded on all sides by water, and they went from one place to another in canoes. This reminded the Spaniards of Venice. So they called the country Venezuela, a word which means "Little Venice," and by this name it has gone ever since. There is a similar town on Maracaibo to-day. The Indians inhabiting it live by fishing. They are quite savage, and although they speak Spanish, they have not united with the whites, as have many other tribes of the country.

Venezuela is also a land of mountains. Branches of the

Andes extend out into it, and we find the capital situated a little back from the seacoast in a nest in the mountains. Many of the mountains contain deposits of gold and other valuable minerals. There are rich gold mines south of the Orinoco, and among them one which has produced more than a million dollars' worth of gold in a year. It is said to be the second richest gold mine of the world.

The chief wealth, however, of Venezuela is in its soil. We have already seen the great pastures, the llanos of the Orinoco basin. There are in the north and northwest vast tracts of rich land, which produces great quantities of fine tobacco, cotton, and coffee.

The coffee plantations are especially interesting. The climate here is warmer than in the coffee lands of southern Brazil, and we find that the trees are raised differently. The most of the fields are irrigated. The coffee trees are shaded to protect them from the sun. The young sprouts are set out among banana plants. The bananas shoot up quickly, and their wide green leaves ward off the rays of the sun from the tender coffee trees, and keep the soil moist. Later, bucuara trees are planted. These trees grow rapidly, and soon extend high above the coffee plants, sending out branches like those of the sycamore, and furnishing just the right shade. The coffee produced in Venezuela is of a very good quality. It is much like mocha coffee, and much of it is sold as mocha in our market.

Along the coast of Venezuela we see many cacao orchards, and learn that they produce very fine chocolate. The trees are carefully cultivated, the orchards being laid out much the same as our peach orchards, save that the trees are protected from the sun in the same way as the coffee trees are. The orchards are also irrigated. The weeds are kept down, and the fruit is more carefully cared for than that of the orchards we saw on the Amazon. The result is that the trees produce large quantities of fruit, six or seven hundred pounds of chocolate seeds being grown in a year on one acre. Many orchards produce two crops a year.

After the seeds are taken out of the pulp and dried they are carried to the seaports and thence shipped to the

Banana Plantation.

markets. The most of the product goes to Spain, France, and Germany, but some is sent to the United States. The cacao seeds are bought by the fanega, a measure holding about a bushel and a half. As much as twenty million pounds have been exported in one year, and for this the people have received about two million dollars.

Caracas is one of the most interesting of the South American capitals. It is the chief city of Venezuela, and although its population is less than one hundred thousand, it is about three times as large as any other town in Venezuela.

Caracas is situated in a little basin on the southern slope of the mountains, only six miles in a straight line back

Statue of Washington.

from the coast. Still, it is more than half a mile high up in the air, and in traveling to it on the railroad we have to go more than twenty-two miles.

We ride through banana fields and palm groves, then climb the mountains, now turning this way, now that. Now we go over bridges with gorges below us which are many hundred feet deep, and now we shoot through tunnels, to come out again on the side of the mountain, with the vast expanse of the Caribbean Sea spread out under our eyes.

The air grows cooler. The yellow-fever-laden, tropical atmosphere of the coast has disappeared, and when at last we land in Caracas we are in one of the most healthful climates of the world.

"We see pretty Spanish women looking out."

The city lies in a beautiful valley, about two miles wide and fifteen miles long, surrounded by mountains, some of which are two miles in height. The valley is covered with sugar plantations, vegetable gardens, coffee groves, and orchards of oranges, lemons, and other fruit.

We are surprised at the city. The streets are narrow, but the sidewalks are made of Portland cement, and the bright buildings facing them are of all colors of the rainbow. They are nearly all of one story and have ridge roofs of red tile. Many of them have windows facing the street, heavily barred, and through the bars we see pretty Spanish women looking out.

The streets cross one another at right angles, with a number of plazas or parks. In one of the parks there is a bronze statue of George Washington, and in another a statue of Simon Bolivar, the hero of Venezuela, and in fact of all South America. He was the Washington of this part of the world. He organized a movement which resulted in the independence of Venezuela, New Granada or Colombia, and Peru, and he was the founder of Bolivia.

Statue of Bolivar.

Later on we visit the Caracas University. We spend some time in the Federal Palace, and also in the Houses of Congress, where we learn that the country is governed in much the same way as our own.

At night we go about the streets under the rays of electric lights. We ride from one part of the city to another on street railways, and notice that Caracas has many of the modern improvements. Many of the young Venezuelans we meet speak English and French, and we see that the better classes of the people live as comfortably as we do at home. Some of them have large one-story houses composed of many rooms encircling courts, or patios, in which grow great rose trees, curious varieties of palms, and all sorts of tropical plants.

In a Garden.

The Venezuelans are very hospitable. They pride themselves upon being one of the most enterprising peoples of the South American continent, and think their country is destined to be the greatest among those of the southern half of our hemisphere.

They are more interested in the United States than the other South Americans. A large part of their trade is with us, and there are fast steamships which start every few days from La Guaira to New York. The journey takes not much more than a week, and as we stand on the wharf and look at the ships flying the American flag we feel inclined to jump on board and go home.

There is, however, another country left to visit. We have the Guianas yet to explore. So we take one of the little steamers which is going east along the coast, and, by changing again at the island of Trinidad, get a ship bound for Georgetown, the capital of British Guiana.

XLIV. IN THE GUIANAS.

THE Guianas are different from the other countries of South America in that they are colonies belonging to nations of Europe. British Guiana belongs to Great Britain, Dutch Guiana is a dependency of Holland, and French Guiana is the property of France. All of these countries have governors appointed by the rulers of the countries to which they belong. None of them have large populations, and as a whole they are of little importance in the commerce and trade of the South American continent.

Still, when South America was discovered this region was thought to be one of the richest of all. It was a part of a country described by the explorers as full of gold, silver, and precious stones. One adventurer who skirted the Guianas and entered the Orinoco told about a city called El Dorado, which had been built in the midst of a great white lake, whose smallest house surpassed in grandeur the palaces of the Incas and Aztecs. "In this city," said the explorer, "the vessels used in the kitchens are of gold and silver, studded with diamonds. The houses have statues of solid gold as big as giants, and there are figures of beasts, birds, fish, and trees, all of gold. The pleasure gardens of the islands are filled with figures of gold and silver, and the king of the country and his court wear clothes of such a nature that they seem to be sprinkled with gold and silver from sandal to crown."

The descriptions of this wonderful city excited all Europe, and expeditions were formed to explore this part of the world. Great numbers of young men left Europe for this purpose, expecting to make fortunes, and in looking for the fabulous city they explored the greater part of northern South America, penetrating to the sources of the Orinoco, entering the Amazon and the rivers which flow out into the Atlantic through the Guianas.

It was from the expedition led or sent by Sir Walter Raleigh that Great Britain became possessed of British Guiana, and it is said that Sir Walter Raleigh presented to Queen Elizabeth some gold nuggets and rude images of solid gold as an evidence of the value of his discovery.

Gold really exists along the Orinoco, the Essequibo, and in some of the streams of French and Dutch Guiana. It has not been discovered in the Guianas, however, in very large quantities, and the wonderful city of El Dorado, with its gold and diamond kitchen utensils, is yet to be found.

The land of the Guianas is of a curious formation. It is a body of highlands, sloping down at its outer edges toward the basin of the Orinoco and that of the Amazon in such a way that if the country were dropped down a few hundred feet the water of the sea would rush in and the Guianas would be a large island.

The exact extent of the territory is not known. French Guiana claims a part of Brazil, and British Guiana has for a long time contended that much of Venezuela should rightly belong to it. At the lowest estimate, however, each of the three countries is as large as the State of New York, and they all contain some excellent land.

The climate of most parts is very unhealthful. It is exceedingly hot, and the highlands are covered with forests as dense as the wildest parts of the Amazon. Here and there are great grassy plains, upon which cattle might be fed, and upon the lowlands near the coast are many places which grow sugar, coffee, and cotton.

But what kind of people are there in these countries? We shall see the civilized population of the coast cities. The majority of the inhabitants, however, live in the wilds. They are savage Indians and savage negroes, the descendants of runaway slaves. The Indians are of many tribes, and they have very strange customs.

The Arawaks, according to report, have a game called the whip dance, in which the dancers stand in two rows opposite each other. Each one has a whip with a hard, strong lash made of fiber. With these they whip the naked calves of each other's legs, often thrashing each other until their legs are covered with blood. The dance is looked upon as a test of endurance and bravery, and the man who can stand the most whipping is considered the best. The game goes on, it is said, with perfect good temper, and at its close the dancers go off in a band and drink one another's health.

The people of another tribe of Indians wear nothing but a strip of cloth about their waists. They are, however, fond of jewelry, and pierce their lower lips in such a way that two pins can be worn in them. They also have pins in their nostrils, and deck their necks and arms with such beads and coins as they can pick up.

The Indians are of many tribes. Some of them paint their bodies, wear bits of bone in their lips, and cause their calves to swell by means of garters tightly clasped below the knee.

There are other strange Indians who are said to have light complexions, with blue eyes and light beards, and rumor gives it that there is a fairy race in these regions which all other Indians dread. Most of these reports come from hearsay, and some of them, like the story of the gold city of El Dorado, may not be true. We have not the time required to make such explorations ourselves, and so shall leave the exact nature of the Indians in doubt, saying we suppose that they may be as reported, but we really do not know.

There is no doubt, however, about there being many black people in the Guianas. We shall see civilized negroes everywhere. Slaves were imported for generations to work on the sugar plantations, and to get the fine woods out of the forests and put them on the ships for Europe. After slavery was abolished many of the negroes settled on the coast lands where they had been toiling. We see their thatched huts everywhere. They are now farmers.

Other negroes went off to the woods and formed tribes of bush negroes, intermarrying with the Indians. The bush negroes have a language which is a mixture of Dutch, French, and English, combined with Indian and African words. Some of the wild negroes are very brave, many being strong and fine-looking.

"We see their thatched huts everywhere."

But here we are at the wharf of Georgetown. We have sailed up a little river, the banks of which are lined with tropical vegetation, with sugar estates cut out of the jungle. We see many cocoanut palms, clumps of bamboos, and great trees covered with flowers.

What a queer crowd is that on the wharf! We rub our

eyes and wonder if we are not in Asia rather than in South America. There are scores of almond-eyed Chinese with their hair hanging in long tails down their backs. There are black Hindoos in turbans and strange garments, and there are Parsees wearing long black coats and hats like inverted coal scuttles. There are numerous Portuguese, and English merchants who have come to the steamer. The most of the Hindoos and Chinese were imported to work on the sugar plantations, and we find them scattered everywhere throughout the coast countries.

"There are black Hindoos in turbans and strange garments."

How queer Georgetown looks after our long stay in the Spanish and Portuguese cities of other parts of the continent! It is more like a city of Holland than Spain. The roofs are slanting, and the walls of most of the houses are of wood or galvanized iron. Many of the houses are tall, built with gable ends facing the street. Near every house is a great iron tank. This is to catch the rain water which is used for drinking, for it is better than that which comes from the springs near the city.

Georgetown has about fifty thousand inhabitants and it has some large buildings. The city lies on low land, and the large buildings stand upon wooden piles which have been driven down into the mud to form the foundations. In many of the streets run canals, which serve to drain the water out into the river in times of flood.

The city has many modern improvements. We enjoy visiting the stores, for the merchants speak English, and we take the tramway and ride out to the suburbs, where the houses stand by themselves in beautiful gardens filled with tropical plants.

The sugar plantations are interesting. Many of them are large, employing hundreds of laborers and making thousands of tons of sugar each season. Each has its manager and overseers, and its books are kept as carefully as those of our great business establishments.

The land of the Guiana coast is so rich that the sugar cane can be cut several times a year, and it is said that it will grow up for sixty years in succession without being replanted. The soil is composed of earth washings brought down by the rivers from the mountains, soil so rich that it will grow everything produced in the tropics. Great quantities of dirt are brought during the floods, which are so great that dikes have to be erected to keep the land from washing into the sea. The building of these dikes is very expensive, and so the sugar plantations are nearly all owned by men and companies having large capital.

We find more sugar plantations near Paramaribo, the capital of Dutch Guiana, which we reach in a little Dutch ship from Georgetown. Paramaribo lies about twenty miles up the Surinam river. It has about thirty thousand inhabitants, and in its architecture and the waterways and houses it is not unlike the cities of Holland

Many of the people speak Dutch, a language which sounds very queer to us when it comes from the negroes we see everywhere. There are also many whites and mulattoes. There are also black-skinned Javanese who have come to work in the sugar plantations. The better classes are dressed in light clothes, the women wearing stiff skirts, loose jackets, and head-dresses not unlike turbans. The poorer people go barefooted, and many of the children wear no clothing whatever.

Cayenne Creole.

From Paramaribo we steam to Cayenne, the capital of French Guiana. The city is smaller than either Georgetown or Paramaribo. It contains about twelve thousand inhabitants, but it looks quite large from the ship, with a grove of palm trees behind it and a high church steeple rising above the rest of the houses.

It is built upon an island about thirty miles in circumference, a narrow strait separating it from the mainland. We find the town interesting. The most of its houses are of two stories, some of them being covered with plaster which is painted all colors of the rainbow.

The land is not much different from that of the other Guianas, and the people are much the same. We see,

In Cayenne.

however, many hard faces among them. French Guiana has for years been a penal colony, to which thieves and other criminals have been exported from France.

Its climate is not healthful, and it is indeed not a place where any traveler would care to stay long. We are glad when the steamer arrives on which we can go back to Trinidad Island, and thence, having finished our long tour of the South American continent, take ship for New York.

INDEX.

Aconcagua, Mount, 73, 82, 122.
Alpacas, 76.
Amazon, 299-327.
Andes, mines of, 95-100.
Andes, in Colombia, 19, 32; Ecuador, 44-46, 50; Peru, 67-80; Chile, 119-122.
Ant cities, 228.
Argentina, 167-200.
Armadillo, 199.
Asuncion, 219-225.

Bahia, 283-290.
Balboa, Vasco Nuñez, discovery of Pacific Ocean, 17.
Bananas, 24, 258.
Beef, dried, 208, 329.
Beef extract factories, Uruguay, 208.
Bodegas, 42, 43.
Bogota, 35-37.
Bolivar, Simon, 340.
Bolivia, 87-100.
Borax, 101.
Brazil, 243-327.
Brazil nut, 323.
Buenos Aires, 192-200.

Cabot, Sebastian, 211.
Cacao, or chocolate, 32-34, 324, 336.
Canal, Panama, 18, 20.
Cape Pilar, 157.
Caracas, 338-341.
Carbons, 290.
Cauca, river and valley, 32-34.
Cayenne, 349.
Ceara, Brazil, 295.
Chile, 100-167.
Chocolate. See *Cacao*.
Chuño, how made, 81.
Cinchona, 92.

Cinnamon trees, 279.
Ciudad Bolivar, 330-333.
Coal mines of Chile, 144-148.
Coca, 93.
Cocoanuts, how grown, 23, 26.
Coffee, 252, 257-267, 271-274, 336.
Colombia, 16-38.
Colon, Isthmus of Panama, 20-22.
Commerce on Lake Titicaca, 84, 85.
Concepcion, 144.
Cordova, 185.
Cuyaba, Brazil, 247.
Cuzco, 77.

Desaguadero, river of, 83.
Desert, Great South American, 50-54, 110.
Diamonds, 288-290.

Earth building in the Parana, 213.
Ecuador, 38-50.
El Dorado, 342.

Farming, in Argentina, 182-190; Brazil, 294; Chile, 130; Paraguay, 226; Peru, 53-55.

Gauchos, the cowboys of the pampas, 179.
Georgetown, 347.
Germans in southern Brazil, 251, 252.
Gold mining, 95, 96, 163, 248.
Guanacos, 169.
Guano, 106.
Guayaquil, 38-42.
Guayas river, 38, 42.
Guianas, 342-350.
Gulf Stream, 14.

Honda, Colombia, 35.
Horses in Argentina, 179.

INDEX.

Iguana lizard, 27.
Incas, the, 77, 78.
Indians, Alacalufes, 154–156; Araucanians, 137–144; Ecuador, 49; Guiana, 344; Peruvian, 69; Quichua and Aymara, 78–80; Onas, 165; Paraguay, 237; Yaghans, 167; Venezuela, 334, 335.
Ipecac, 248.
Iquique, 102.

Llamas, 75, 76.
Llanos, 328, 329.
La Paz, 87–92.
Lima, 58–66.
Locusts, 188, 189.

Magdalena river, 35.
Magellan, Strait of, 149, 151–167.
Manaos, 325–327.
Manioc, how raised, 225.
Mate, or Paraguay tea, 234.
Matto Grosso, Brazil, 242, 249.
Montevideo, 203–208.
Mountain sickness, 71.

Negroes, in Brazil, 285–287; in the Guianas, 345, 346.
Nitrate of soda, 101–105.

Obidos, 324.
Oranges in Paraguay, 231.
Orinoco river, 327–334.
Oroya Railroad, 67.
Ostriches, 170.

Palms, ivory, 25; cocoanut, 26; royal, 278; carnauba, 298.
Pampas, 169–174.
Panama, 28.
Panama, Isthmus of, 16–29.
Panama Canal, 18, 20.
Panama Railroad, 24.
Para, 305–312.
Paraguay, 217–249.
Paraguay river, 216, 233–248.
Paramaribo, 349.
Parana river, 212–216.
Parrots, 298.
Passport, 11, 12.
Patagonia, 167.
Peccary, 240.

Pernambuco, 291.
Peru, 50–86.
Petropolis, 282.
Pizarro, 58.
Plateau of Peru, 72–80.
Poopo, Lake, 83.
Potatoes, 81.
Punta Arenas, 159–162.

Quinine, 92.
Quinua, 74.
Quito, 47.

Railroads, Brazil, 254, 267, 281; Peru, 67; Transandine, 115–122, 169.
Recife, 291.
Rio de Janeiro, 267–280.
Rio de la Plata, 208.
Rio Negro, Brazil, 325.
Rosario, 191.
Rotos, or Chilean workmen, 135.
Rubber, 312–320.

San Salvador, 15.
Santiago, 123–130.
Santos, 252, 253.
São Paulo, 255.
Sheep freezing, 176.
Sheep raising, 164, 174.
Silver, 97, 108.
Smythes Channel, 151.
Spaniards in South America, 57, 58, 77.
Stock raising in Argentina, 177.
Sugar cane, 54, 183, 348.

Tapir, 241.
Tierra del Fuego, 162–167.
Tin, 99.
Titicaca, Lake, 81–86.
Turtles, 311, 312.

Uruguay, 201–208.

Valparaiso, 109, 112.
Venezuela, 327–342.
Vicuña, 76.
Vineyards, 184.
Vultures, 310.

Wheat in Argentina, 187–192.
Wool, 197. See also *Sheep*.

www.ingramcontent.com/pod-product-compliance
Lightning Source LLC
Chambersburg PA
CBHW030307240426
43673CB00040B/1086